TO MY PARENTS

SPEEDSEEKERS

I am a speed seeker, and I guess I always have been. I've been fascinated by hot rod and custom car culture ever since I was a young girl playing with Hot Wheels instead of Barbie Dolls. As a teenager I became interested in rock n' roll and by the age of 14 was rocking out in a band. This led to a surf band and then an all girl punk band. Through the music I became more and more aware of car culture and the magnetic pull it exerted on me. Once I was old enough I began purchasing vintage cars and motorcycles.

I began to photograph cars, write stories and collect hot rod paraphernalia. The world I was discovering so deeply affected me that a need to share this world with others took hold. By 1997 I had started to work on the concepts that would eventually become *Speedseekers*. Hungry for information and images I came across the book *Hot Rod* by David Perry and was so inspired I decided to contact him. David and his wife Mary suggested I come with them to Bonneville for Speed Week. There was no way I could resist. I packed my bags and flew to Salt Lake City to meet my future mentor at a truck stop next to Bonneville.

Ever since that first trip I have returned to the United States and traveled the world to experience car culture firsthand. I have kept my eyes and ears open on the streets of Los Angeles, at the racetracks, the dry lakes, the salt, and in the homes and garages of the originators of this culture, and of those that followed in their footsteps. This book is the result of those years spent in the heart of a culture I love and respect.

Alexandra Lier, August 2008

SPEEDSEEKERS

THE SUPERCHARGED WORLD OF CUSTOM CARS AND HOT RODS

ALEXANDRA LIER

WITH TEXTS BY KEVIN THOMSON

Thames & Hudson

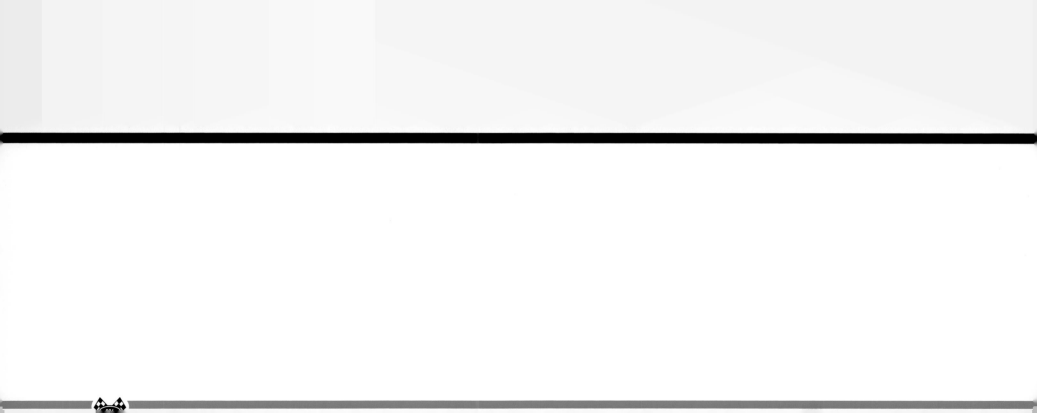

HISTORY

A few hours before sunrise and some sealed beams light up the brush on either side of the narrow blacktop. Few people if any live out here and the road is seldom traveled. There are no clusters of light denoting factory, mall, or home in the night. Behind the first headlights, other pairs of lights are strung along the highway. No one sees them. The only sound is the drone of the machinery that powers them.

The mountain ranges become spread out, looming far off under starlight and beams of a young moon. In between the peaks, the road travels the valley before stabbing North onto dirt. Jackrabbits freeze in the lights then dart into the sage and creosote. The vegetation thins then ends. What was once a verdant underwater paradise lays void of all creatures or plants, wide open and glowing.

First dawn finds them all there. Busy. Removing fenders and windshields, testing new inventions, getting ready to see just how much speed the old lakebed and their machinery will allow. Some of these cars see daily street service and might never pass for a real "gow job". When the fenders come off, the bumper is ditched, and the three-carb manifold is bolted to the flathead, the character is decidedly changed. Full sun sees a course laid out

and the dust rising. Open exhausts at tenor pitch ring out for the length of the three miles. Sometimes they go three and four abreast until the practice is recognized as insane. From then on it is one at a time against the clock. It's a dangerous affair and even under the best circumstances, still is today.

By nightfall the group is camped. Fires for cooking, drinking and talking are burning. Notes are compared, records discussed, stories swapped. Several are hard at work by lantern, repairing or improving their machinery. No time for sidetracks, and sleep is a luxury when a record or just getting home is at stake. The Mojave might be a long drive from Kansas but it's an even further walk back to Los Angeles. There was no "coverage" out there in the California desert back then, there wasn't a happy burger, double frosted iced crappacino or an ambulance for miles. What these early hotrodders did was double or nothing, your life on the line. Defying life and limb for speed and peer recognition, they created an ethic and style that has been consumed, regurgitated and sold again and again. In the core, beyond the reach of studio lighting, the story of the early twentieth century lakes racer remains the genesis of hot rod history.

1997

Andy Green breaks the sound barrier with "Thrust SSC" at Black Rock Desert.

1940

A pre-war hot rod '29 Ford roadster ready for the Dry Lakes.

Hotrodding started in the United States in the 1920s. The mass-produced, affordable automobile, like the FORD MODEL T, gave rise to this new culture. As the wrecks piled up in the yards of the newly-formed auto salvage business, a veritable grab bag of cheap parts and bodies became available to the would-be hotrodder seeking to create a "gow job". Speed secrets traveled low to the ground like gasoline vapors leaking from the garages of racers, gangsters, whiskey runners, machinists, and inventors into the minds and out of the hands of young men bent on going fast. Inevitably, experimentation spread faster than fleas in a barnyard. Bodies and frames of different models or makes found new lives together and their engines became "hopped up". With the introduction of the new FORD MODEL A in 1927 and the new FORD flathead V-8 three- and five-window coupes in 1932, the die was cast.

The dry lakes of the Mojave Desert were a relatively short country drive from the greater Los Angeles area of the 1930s and they quickly became the venue of choice for hotrodders to race each other and the clock. It was here at the lakes that the definitive hot rod took shape. Bodies were stripped of their fenders, windshields chopped down or removed, louvers were punched into the bodies (to allow air to escape), and taller rear tires were fitted to improve top end speed. The engines became further modified with multiple carburetors, "stroker" crankshafts (to increase displacement), specially ground camshafts and modified cylinder heads.

By the time World War II broke out roadsters were running the lakes at over 120 mph and hotrodding had become an established subculture. By now, there were millions of cars on the road in the U.S. and car culture had taken hold. Entrepreneurs of all kinds sprang up to meet the demands of the motoring public. Cheap and fast roadside food, motels, and dual-carb manifolds were entering the public consciousness.

World War II took a grueling and painful bite out of the hot rod timeline. Young American servicemen returning home from the war in 1945 wasted no time in picking up where they had left off in 1941, and hotrodding was back full bore. Many of the guys had worked as mechanics in the service, where they honed or learned skills they would put to use on their cars. The use of nitrous oxide and nitro methane to boost power crossed over to hot rods from the aircraft industry. Action was heavy again out at the lakes, but hotrodding was quickly becoming a nationwide phenomenon and street racing was becoming both a public nuisance and a symbol of youth culture gone haywire.

In 1949 two major events happened which conferred legitimacy in the public eye to hotrodding. One was the first-ever Speed Week held at the Bonneville Salt Flats in Utah, and the other was the first organized drag race held by permission of the police department on a half-mile section of road in Goleta, California. Bonneville would become the Holy Land of the speed afflicted but the drag race in Goleta started a whole new game. 1950 saw the first commercial dragstrip open in Santa Ana, California and more were soon to follow throughout the country. By the end of the decade, drag racing would become a major spectator sport with its own subculture, technology and stars.

The drags emphasized quick acceleration and the form of the cars began to follow this function. Weight is the enemy. In 1950 Dick Kraft tore everything off his car and created his "bug". The bug was recognized as the first "rail job". Crude and effective, the "bug" was nothing more than frame rails with a seat and an engine. Drag racing in the 1950s was an experimental affair and by 1959 the rail job was a slingshot: a tube framed, narrow-bodied, front-engined, lightweight machine with the driver perched behind the rear wheels, first perfected by Mickey Thompson. This design would be further refined until the old idea of a rear engine came back with a vengeance in the guise of Don Garlits' rear-engined ride in 1971. Vying for popularity alongside the rails were the gassers and the hot rod flavored altereds. These cars were nearly out of control and put on a show to rival the rail jobs.

Hot Wheels™

Servicemen return from the war and hotrodding takes off again.

1945

GA

Ray Brown's rear-engine, flathead V-8 powered, '27 MODEL T class A roadster placed 1st in the May 1951 Russetta meet with a speed of 124.309 mph.

1992

The barebones, traditional hot rods make a comeback. Top fuel breaks 300 mph.

1974

Top fuel puts the motor behind the driver. The oil embargo continues as custom vans rule the street and factory muscle cars die off.

On the streets a new breed had taken up the art of transforming everyday rides into street-scene mind blowers. The new kustomizers could see right through the designs Detroit gave them, and built what they saw in their own minds. Tops were chopped not to improve speed, but to improve the look. Paint became a science of its own with the introduction of candies, pearls and metal flake. Hotrodding was branching out, transforming itself into different niches of the same underlying philosophy of 'do-it-yourself innovation. Detroit couldn't help but notice and in 1955 Chrysler spat out the 300, so named for its 300 horsepower 331-cubic inch Hemi engine. The "factory hot rod", or "muscle car" had just pulled into town.

The stock and super stock classes began turning into the big show at the drags by 1960. This was where everybody could see a car like the one they drive every day tear up the track, and it was pure 'gearhead' inspiration. The factories were in a heat to out-do each other. What looked innocent enough on the outside was packin' big cubes and plenty of HP. By the mid-sixties the muscle car was evident on the streets, but the true factory hot rods were getting further and further away from their family transport roots. Dual Quad Chevy 427's, "swiss cheese" 1963 Pontiac Catalinas, and 12.5:1 compression ratio 426 Hemis evolved into the A/FX or factory experimental class that started a Mercury vs. Mopar showdown. This all

culminated in the illogical/logical conclusion of the Altered Wheelbase 1965 Dodge and Plymouths which the fans and press dubbed, "funny cars"... hardly the car to take the kids to the pool in. These cars gave rise to the first true flopper in 1966. Given the green light by Al Turner, head of the Mercury race effort, Ron and Gene Logghe produced a tube frame chassis with the driver seated in the middle and behind the radically set back engine. The body was one piece of fiberglass molded in the shape of a 1966 Mercury Comet, which was hinged at the rear to lift off the chassis. This new species of funny car blew the doors off the previous funnies that still had their doors in place. Off the trailer and through the lights the Comets ran in the 8-second range, an epic second off the previous best "funny car" times. Hotrodding and customizing kept right on going throughout the sixties despite the muscle car's popularity. For the hotrodder, different body styles were gaining acceptance, although the purist might insist on a roadster. The new tricks included cool aftermarket rims and even more parts borrowed from the race crowd. The hot rod still had to have its go, and the aftermarket and Detroit kept a steady supply of that on hand. Cheap, high-octane fuel made tough compression ratios the norm and the typical true hot rod engine of the sixties had a nasty exhaust note due to those high compression ratios coupled with radically profiled camshafts. On the other side the customs were keeping

the engines relatively mild with more flash and chrome (despite the occasional blower) than having true speed parts in the mix. The reason was that you just didn't need 12:1 pistons to make the scene in your sled. What you needed was a keen sense of which parts to mix and match along with which lines to emphasize or de-emphasize to make your creation stand above the "mild" customs. Around this time the average "drive-in burger stand" hotrodder began to borrow more from the custom crowd and the "street rod" was beginning to make the scene in growing numbers. The street rod might have some of the look of the true hot rod but more often than not the engine was milder and "mod cons" like power steering, and power brakes made the street rod totally different from a true hot rod. The lines were at once blurring and at the same time being drawn.

In 1971 the movie *Two Lane Blacktop* was released and the line between the factory ride and the homegrown rod was made perfectly clear for all to see. In the movie, a new GTO driven by Warren Oates engages in a cross-country race with a homebuilt, primered, '55 Chevy racer (the car) piloted by James Taylor (the driver) and Dennis Wilson (the mechanic).

Wilson and Taylor make their way aimlessly by street racing for a living. Warren Oates is a

loner with a mid-life crisis going nowhere "fast or too fast". Despite the film's heavy existentialist vibe, there is no way to miss the point that the GTO might be fast, but it's got no soul compared to the primered '55 Chevy, which represents the sum total of the lives of The Driver and The Mechanic.

On the dragstrips of the early seventies the show was getting wilder in line with the times, and televised drag racing was becoming "big bucks" in every way. Corporate sponsorship as well as showmanship was all-important. A prime example of show and speed was the funny car team of "Jungle" Jim Lieberman and his teammate "Jungle" Pam Hardy. Jungle was one of the best drivers and tuners of his time and was extremely competitive despite a lifestyle that epitomized the sex, drugs, and rock n' roll paradigm of the early 1970s. Funny cars were only part of the fastest show on earth. Super stocks evolved into pro stocks, and top fuel put the motor behind the driver for good. Speeds immediately went up and ET's went down once the combos were sorted. Just when it seemed like it was going to last forever, the oil embargo hit and custom vans became the rage. *Rod and Custom* magazine folded into the pages of *Hot Rod* magazine and the light was getting dim. Despite all the darkness, the hardcore kept the torches lit and tops kept being chopped and engines became even more powerful.

1969

The factory muscle car war heats up with more models and engines available than ever before.

By the end of the seventies about the only thing happening was punk rock. The muscle car was finished, disco was dying a slow death and then along came the eighties. Neon monochrome paint jobs, the birth of billet, Boyd Coddington, splash graphics, and ZZ Top's "Eliminator" set the hot rod tone for the eighties. The popularity of the movement was proven by National Street Rod Association shows that had grown into 15,000-car monster events. The mid eighties saw the rebirth of the muscle car and the rise of a new movement called "pro-street". Pro-street took a '60s or '70s car (anything really) and built a near cartoon version of a full-blown drag car meant to be driven on the street. The muscle car came back as a collectible and prices for rare original examples soared in response. This in turn began an after-market of restoration parts and upgrades for these now older cars. The interest spilled over into more speed parts and muscle cars began appearing in numbers not seen since the sixties.

A nostalgic turn began simmering in the hot rod, custom and drag world towards the end of the eighties. Perhaps this turn towards the past was a reaction against all the perfection, flash and money in the hot rod, drag, pro-street and muscle car world or maybe it was just the normal course of events. Whatever the case, hot rods in primer, "rare" muscle cars being abused on the strip, and front-motored rail jobs were coming back.

Across the board the nineties represented the buildup to the car culture we have in the first decade of the 21st century. In the underground rock and art world the fascination with Auto-Americana was represented by lyrical content, graphic style, fashion, and ownership of a vintage ride: muscle car, hot rod custom, or cruiser/beater. Long forgotten car clubs were resurrected and the first "Billet Proof" show paid homage to builders of traditional home-built rough-and-ready hot rods and customs. Fanzines devoted to the cause like *Speed Kills* and *Gearhead* covered the different aspects of the movement, music and culture. Books like *Kustom Kulture* and *High Performance* were published with more coming hot on their heels. Websites devoted to hotrodding as much as pure nostalgia began to appear.

Nostalgia drag racing featured by the Good Guys on the West Coast took off. Suddenly '60s- and '70s-style race cars were being rebuilt or built from the ground up. Older race cars were now objects worthy of restoration and many continue to be restored and trotted out to be fired up for a few minutes at events like the "Cackle Fest". A resurgence of interest in landspeed racing out on the salt and at the lakes has kept the old tradition of going fast going stronger than ever. Muscle cars, "badged or cloned", kept turning up on the streets and pro-street morphed into a car you could drive, which the magazines dubbed "pro touring". Big brakes, stiff suspensions, low profile tires, plenty of V-8 power, a '60s or early '70s Detroit skin, and the occasional "euro" styling cue became the hallmarks of the pro touring ride at the turn of the century.

Now, in 2008, hotrodding is as mainstream as it can be and the underground is more a force than ever. Car shows now include bands, burlesque shows, clothing, art, and tattoos along with the traditional "show-n-shine" and swap meet. You can build a roadster from the ground up with reproduction parts and a credit card. Nearly any make of muscle car can be resurrected with a phone call to the resto parts houses. Any vision you can conjure up can be built thanks to the aftermarket. Information and advice is just a keystroke away on the Internet. Compared to the days of scrounge and sweat it almost seems easy. Life is good for the hot rod junky and the pedal ain't even hit the metal yet.

1966

Fiberglass-bodied **MERCURY COMET**. The first of the "floppers".

The slingshot had become the standard design for top fuel dragsters.

BY 1959

Stock automobiles start to tear up the dragstrip in stock and super stock classes.

1962

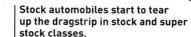

THIRD ANNUAL *Bonneville*
NATIONAL SPEED TRIALS
PRESENTED BY SOUTHERN CALIFORNIA TIMING ASSOCIATION

HELL ON WHEELS!

This Ford Deuce roadster was built, owned and raced by Roadrunners member Ray Brown in 1946. The flathead engine was bored and stroked with Jahns pistons, 9.5 to 1 compression ratio heads, Clay Smith super race cam, an Eddie Meyer dual intake manifold and homemade headers. It turned 123.87 mph.

George Hill's and Bill Davis' streamliner driven by Otto Ryssman at Bonneville in 1953. This car went as fast as 232 mph.

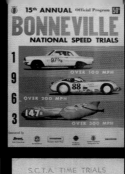

Left: Dick Kraft's primitive "Bug", considered by many to be the very first dragster, gave birth to the moniker "rail job". **Right:** This shot was taken at the SCTA's first official drag race at the Santa Ana, California blimp base on July 2, 1950. The sizeable crowd was just a hint of what was soon to come. The event was co-sponsored by the American Motorcycle Association. These two highboy roadsters, a MODEL A on the left and a '32 FORD on the right, wait to be flagged off by the starter.

The "Mondello-Matsubara" fuel-altered vehicle was one of the better known altereds of the day from Southern California. In this shot "Mondello-Matsubara" is matched against the "Plain Vanilla" car of Charlie Smith from back East. The "Mondello-Matsubara" was the first fuel-altered to break the 200 mph barrier.

Gasser wars at their best. This photo taken at Pomona in 1965 shows the "Stone-Woods-Cook" coupe against the "Mallicoat", Willys coupe. Stone Woods and Cook had the car to beat at the time in their class. The Mallicoats are still racing today in their A/GS nostalgia Barracuda.

Left: Top Eliminator race at Salinas Airport, California, in 1965. An old-style dragstrip with flagman, one spectator side and no return road. The races had to be stopped so cars could come up the race track to get to the pit area. **Right:** The late Dwight "Hay" Bale waits at the start to race his top fueler "Purple Haze". The mask was the latest in protection should the nitro methane-fueled Hemi directly in front of the driver explode.

National DRAGSTER NEWS
FIA Status For NHRA

Winternationals Field Growing

DRAG NEWS

National DRAGSTER
BONUS BUCKS

NHRA Winston
World Championship Series
$100,000.00 SEASON POINTS FUND

NEW SPONSOR FOR '75

DRAG NEWS

DRAG NEWS

springnationals PHOTO REVIEW
National DRAGSTER

UPSETS A PLENTY AT LUBBOCK WCS EVENT

Panter's S/S Win Thrills Canadians At Mission WCS

Ruth, Goodell, & Van Cleave Score in Northwest

National DRAGSTER NEWS
PARKS IS ELECTED ACCUS VP

ALLEN STOPS SURFERS BID FOR CIRCUIT JACKPOT WIN

DRAG NEWS

National DRAGSTER
Snake Blasts 257.35 MPH

ARMY

ABC-TV WINTERNATIONALS
Sunday, February 13th

DRAG NEWS

DRAG NEWS
NO. 1

National DRAGSTER
Season's Greetings

Left: Wild Willie Borsch in the "Winged Express". Willie became famous for the often sideways attitude the car took when doing burnouts and also for his one-armed driving style which later evolved into a gag in which a phony arm was placed atop the side of the door. **Right:** The Kohler Brothers' "King Kong" 1951 FORD Anglia gasser pulling the wheels up on a hard launch. **Overleaf: (L)** The staging lanes at Indy circa 1964. The fuel dragster of Crossley and Williams, the "Kamikaze Car", is the first in line. The lineup of diggers was typical of the regional cars that would show up at a National event during the 1960s.

Above: Bob Riggle in the second generation "Hemi Under Glass" 1968 BARRACUDA wheelstander. Bob would run the entire quarter with the wheels up and sparks flying in under 11 seconds. **Overleaf: (L)** Butter & Girrard top fuel dragster, Irwindale 1968, a favorite local team. **(R)** A spectacular wheelstand at Famoso in 1969, not what you usually want from your top fueler.

Left: Pat Foster about to test-drive Woody Gilmore's first rear-engined dragster, owned by Leland Kolb and George Peloquin, in 1970 at Lions Dragstrip. The steering ratio was too quick and the car suffered a major crash injuring Pat. **Right:** John Dearmore's top fuel car stalling while trying to do a fire burnout, 1970. They are trying to get the car off the track. **Overleaf:** "TV" Tommy Ivo in his first rear-engined dragster doing a fire burnout. Tommy became the first to run an ET – "elapsed time" – in the 5-second range in 1972. Ivo built 32 cars over the course of his career.

VHT
TOMMY IVO
GOODYEAR
zoom
autolite
develco
valvoline
dzus

1961 PONTIAC CATALINA

"7-11 3rd" was the runner-up in its class at the '62 NHRA Nationals at Indianapolis.

Jack Chrisman's 1964 Comet was built specifically to beat the threat of Chrysler's exhibition cars. Chrysler cars were easily beat because the Comet packed the sport's first-blown, injected, nitro-burning motor into a standard American sedan. Jack went on to play a major role in the development of funny cars.

Left: Dyno Don Nicholson and his new 1967 fiberglass-bodied Mercury Cyclone funny car. This is essentially a front-engine dragster with a sedan body hinged at the rear, capable of low 8-second elapsed times in the quarter-mile. **Right: 1** - Crazy topless version of the 1965 Plymouth Belvedere nitro funny car, the "Melrose Missile". This is an extreme example of a steel-bodied car shedding body parts to get weight down. **2** - Arnie Beswick's "Tameless Tiger" altered wheelbase, steel-bodied Pontiac Tempest funny car in 1966. **3** - Nelson Carter's "Super Chief", fiberglass Charger-bodied funny car with nitro-burning Keith Black Hemi in 1972. **4** - Don Cook's "Damn Yankee" fiberglass tilt-bodied 'Cuda built and driven by Pat Foster. This car is what is known as a flopper.

Left: Jungle Jim Lieberman proudly poses with his all-new 1966 Cʜᴇᴠʏ Nᴏᴠᴀ funny car in San Jose, California in 1966. **Right:** Jungle Jim and Jungle Pam Hardy at the starting line in 1973. Pam is checking for oil leaks and psyches the competition. These two were especially emblematic of the sex, drugs and rock n' roll atmosphere of the early 1970s.

The last funny car race at Long Beach in 1972 with a classic match-up of the "Mongoose" (Tom McEwen) vs. the "Snake" (Don Prudhomme) in their Hot Wheels-sponsored funny cars.

Don Cook's "Damn Yankee" 'Cuda funny car ready to launch at Long Beach in 1971.

Above: With their tilt-up bodies and outrageous paint jobs the funny cars of the early 1970s were a real crowd pleaser.
Right: "Lil' John Vega". John Lombardo-Steve Pleuger 1971 VEGA, Donovan-engined funny car.

Left: (above) Tom McEwen's 1978 "English Leather" Corvette funny car. **(below)** Kenny Bernstein's 1987 Buick funny car, the "Bernstein Batmobile", so-called for its advanced aerodynamic design. **Right:** Funny car king, John Force, in his 1987 Oldsmobile funny car at Englishtown, New Jersey. John would go on to win 14 world championships in the funny car class, all under the Castrol banner.

GARAGE

It's the "way" station. The place where you go in between the episodes that make up the rest of your life. Cut on the lights in here and the rest of the world goes dark. Just the way it was the last time you left it, consistent in that respect. Pictures, books, tools, a car, a mess of your own making. A chair for daydreaming, or taking stock. There is an odor of industry, fuel, grease, cut steel. The selection of hammers alone conveys that things can and will be done here.

Parts lay forgotten until a desperate need arises and they are found, dusted off and pressed into service. Bulging cardboard boxes, stacks of wheels, a clutter of carburetors, sheet metal hung like wall art, and bare iron engine blocks signify the working garage. The garage facilitates the art of hoarding. Those with a knack for it will fill all available space from floor to ceiling. The entire stash acts as a kind of palette for the hot rodder to pick and choose from.

Decisions based on line and power are made. Work is begun, hard and frequently dangerous work. The hands are especially vulnerable. The hands are the primary tool and bear the look of it. They are always scarred and

with age they gnarl. With luck they retain five to ten digits. Gloves help, but sometimes the steel is too hot, the tool too slick, or the blade is too fast. This isn't flower arranging, it's a car and it must be built.

The work gets done in bouts that can take years and break marriages. The deadlines in this garage are self-imposed. Clock and calendar lose their status as measuring devices and the car becomes the de facto timepiece here. The car is the prime motivator. It's why you're here, where your time and money go. At your hand the car changes. Each move is one towards completion. The reward is driving the machine you built. The garage then waits for the lights to cut on and the next project to roll in.

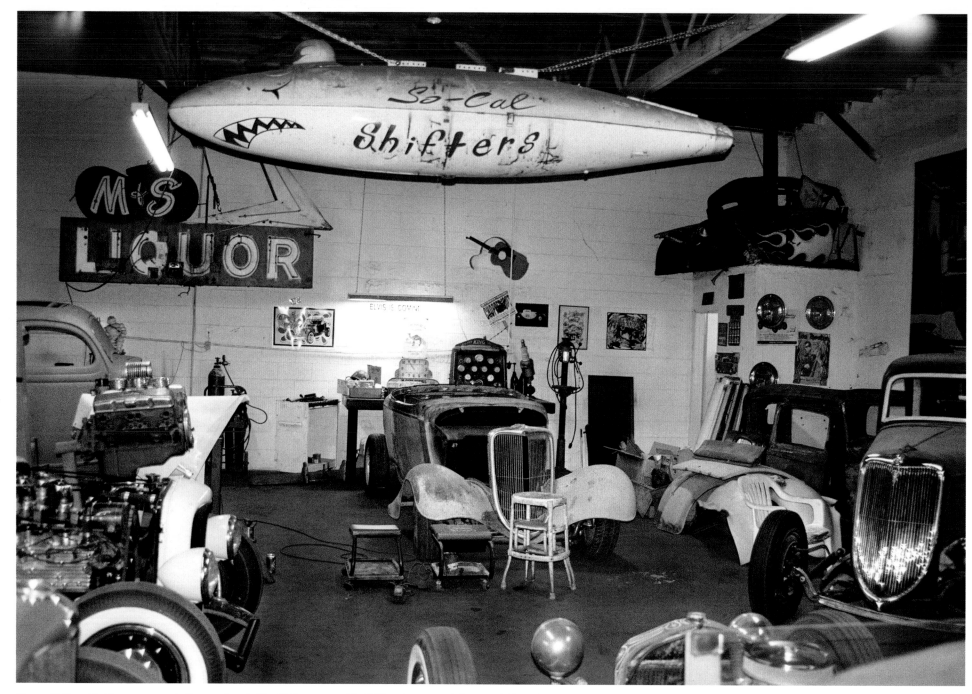

Above: Shifters Clubhouse garage in Orange County. The Shifters started in 1992 and are one of the most influential car clubs to come out of the Southern California hot rod and rockabilly scene. **Right:** From left to right: Jeff, Anthony, Kevin, and friend Nick in the Shifters Clubhouse.
Previous page: Marky Idzardi and his "Purple People Eater".

Kurt Stockman of Taupo, New Zealand and his collection of Petromobilia.

BIG TREE GREASE

AUTOLINE SUPER SAE 40

SHELL TRANSMISSION OIL

GOLDEN FLEECE

EUROPA-LUBE MOTOR OIL

GARGOYLE GREASE

BIG TREE MOTOR No. 3 GREASE

GARGOYLE GREASE NO. 2

CASTROL MOTOR OIL

Left: Tommy, Klaus & Dan moving Tommy's '41 Ford truck cab in Bakersfield, California. **Right:** Tom Herrera's '59 Ford Thunderbird, 352-c.i. V8, with '57 Mercury grille, frenched and extended headlights, and reshaped hoodscoop.

Salinas Boys owner Cole Foster with the 1936 Ford coupe he built for Metallica guitarist Kirk Hammett. The car started out as a five-window, which Cole and the boys chopped and turned into a three-window.

CUSTOMIZIN'
CARS, VANS, CYCLES
INSIDE & OUT!

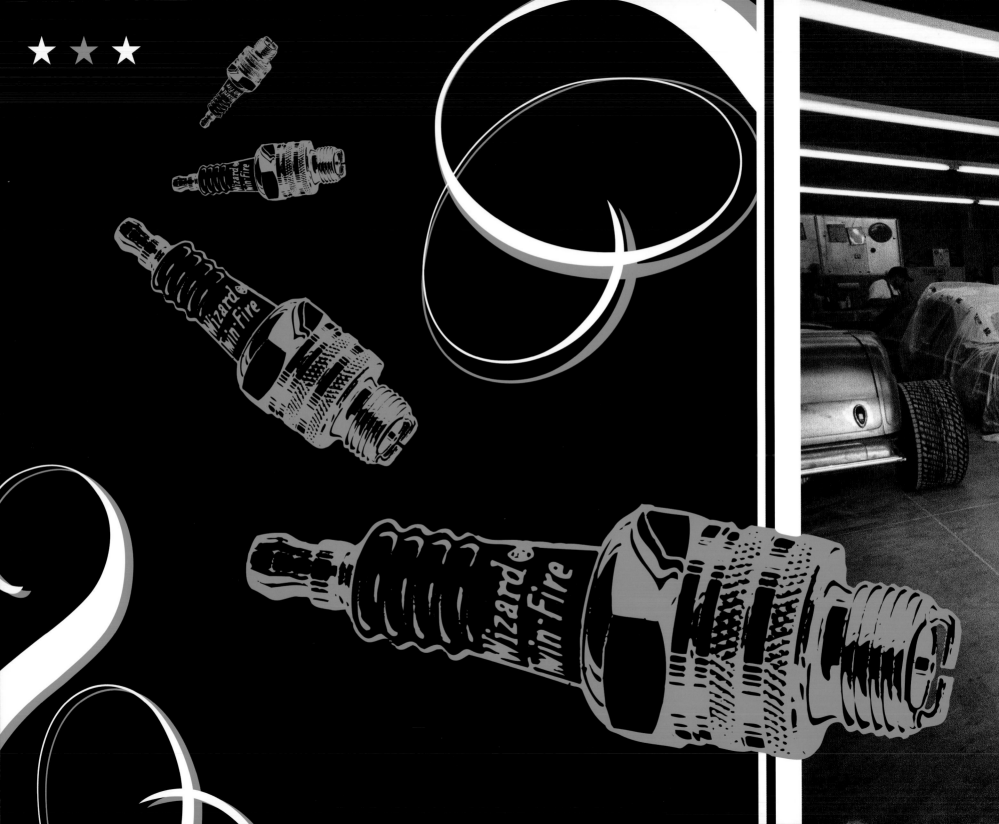

Left: Gene Winfield's Mojave Desert shop, Winfield's Rod & Custom Construction. Gene Winfield has been racing and customizing cars since the 1940s. He is still going strong into his eighties and remains one of the most influential builders of all time. **Right:** Gene Winfield with his Model T lakes racer.

Scott Mugford of Blue Collar Customs in Sacramento with his slammed 1968 PLYMOUTH FURY wagon with a 440 engine. Custom paint by The Gozz. Blue Collar specializes in rods and customs with a traditional look and lots of power.

Above: Shop interior at Blue Collar Customs in Sacramento, California, where traditional hot rods and customs are built. **Overleaf: (L)** All in a day's work at Blue Collar Customs. **(R)** Scott Mugford working metal on an English wheel.

Left: Anthony's shop. **Right:** Greg Coddington and his T-Bucket built by Anthony of The Shifters. **Overleaf:** Brandon Casquilho with his motorcycle "Tiny Dancer". "All the parts are pretty much handmade. It took me two years to build this motorcycle. The true heroes that keep it all going, will one day receive glory in heaven!"

Tiny Dancer

Left & Right: Dan Druff (Los Angeles) with his 1950 Triumph bobber, chrome frame, matching numbers, iron head, everything rebuilt (some things twice). Dan says the bike is faster than it needs to be and took one year to build. He also has a 1967 Dodge Dart GT. **Overleaf: (L)** Bruce Gossett's silkscreen shop in Sacramento where "the studio and the garage collide". **(R)** Bruce with his '54 Plymouth Savoy.

Left: Greg and JoAnn Carlson are active members of the SCTA who also race every year on the Salt at Bonneville. Greg is holding a trophy for fastest time in class.
Right: Interior of the Carlsons' garage with their race cars.

Left: Rod Powell and his garage in Salinas, California where he works his magic with "one shot". **Right:** Interior of Rod Powell's garage.
Overleaf: (L) 1957 DE SOTO at Squeak's shop at Bakersfield. **(R)** Chopped '32 FORD at Squeak Bell's shop.

Nick Haprov working on his 1929 MODEL A roadster pick-up. The little truck started out as a sedan body that had its roof cut off and then cut in half. "I bought it in 2001 from a friend of my brother who needed some cash. The frame is a custom home-made frame that's been drilled out, the motor is a 1955 Ford 239 y-block with the stock 3-speed tranny, and the paint was done by my brother."

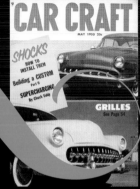

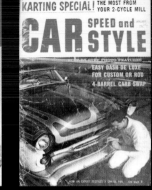

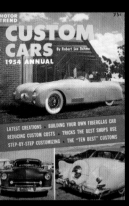

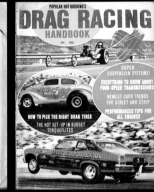

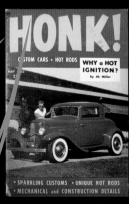

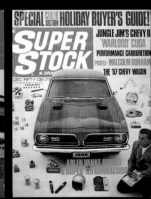

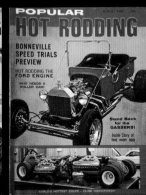

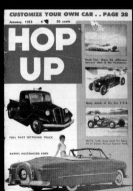

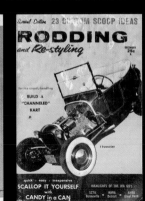

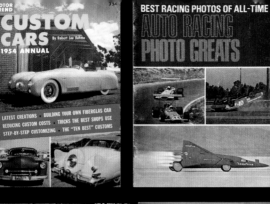

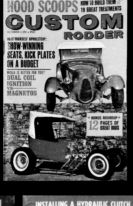

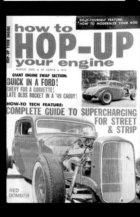

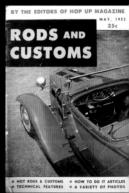
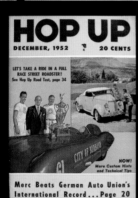

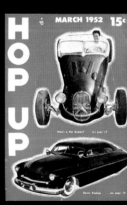

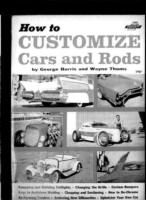

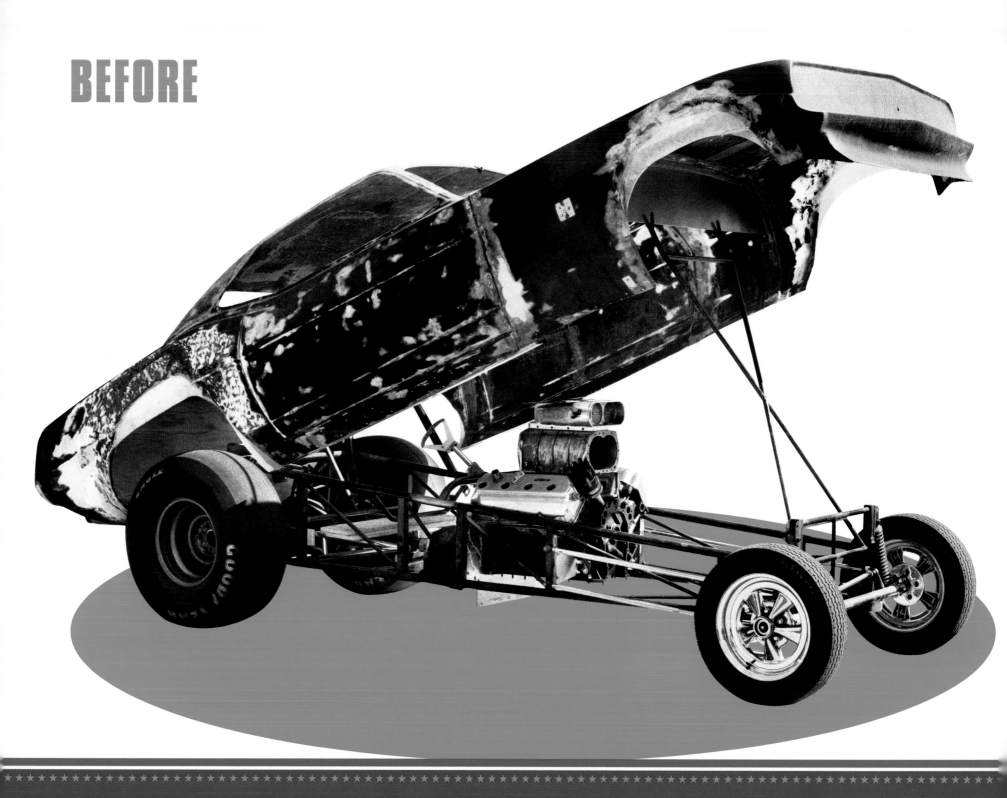

BEFORE

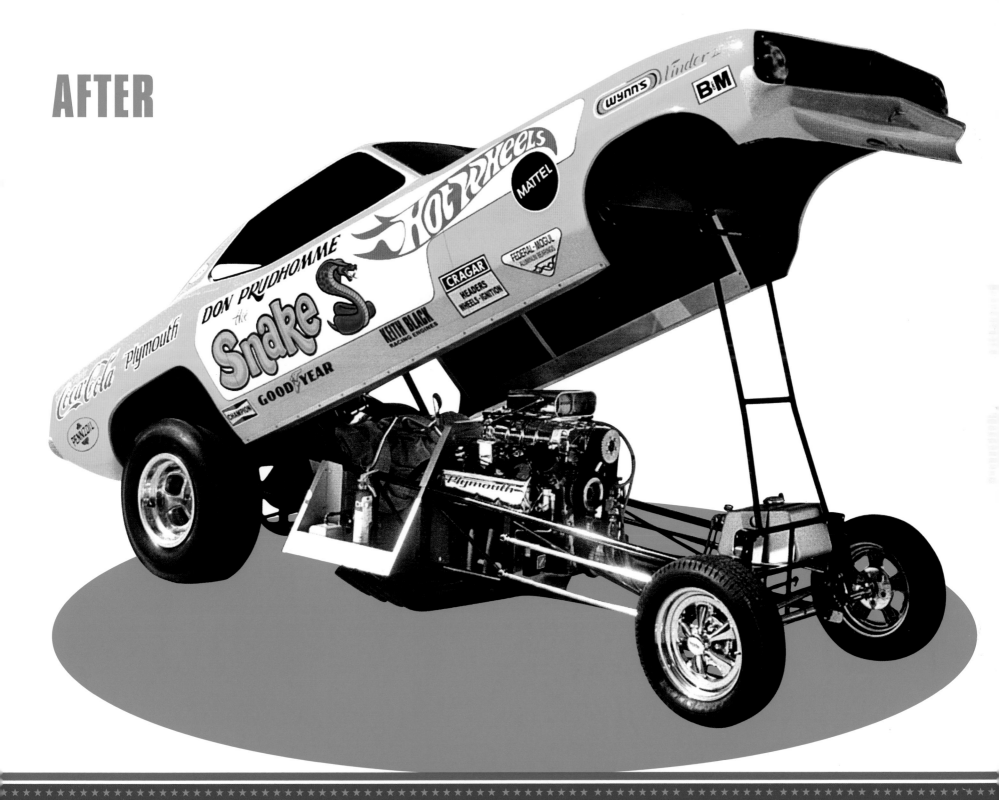

AFTER

Left & Right: Russ Wright of The Demonics, with his 1969 Dodge Super Bee in Daly City, California. Russel says this 440 powered, 1969 Super Bee "is my religion".

Left: Backyard at the Kennedy Brothers shop in Pomona, California. Traditional building methods and meticulous attention to detail have won the Kennedy Brothers a steady clientele. **Right:** Joe and Jason Kennedy with their collection of automobilia and antique surfboards.

Kevin Thomson of Demon Motors cruising his 1966 PLYMOUTH SATELLITE through San Francisco.

1965 Belvedere under construction at Demon Motors in San Francisco.

SPEED

The hands on the wheel begin to tighten as the blood drains from the knuckles. The muted hum of cruise has become the rising pitch of power. He's edgy in his seat. Telephone poles and mile markers whip past the side-glass, then multiply and diminish in the rearview mirror. A solitary, oncoming car appears on the horizon, looms, blurs, and becomes a part of the rapidly disappearing past.

The tachometer reads 5000 rpm. The driver does a mental calculation and figures they're travelling at ten past a ton on a public highway, miles away from anything or anyone. A slip here and they are likely to eat enough sagebrush and dust to die. The passenger squints into the windshield then tries to take in the view from the side-glass. He's a mess of sweat but the driver appears to be cool. The knuckles are drained but her face calm. No

betrayal of velocity. He gets his nerve and nonchalantly asks, "How fast are we going? Is this really fast?" The driver rolls her eyes in response then tromps the pedal. She says, "not until the valves float." The old V-8 gets up around a steady six grand and there's protest, but not from the valves. "C'mon. OK. You're gonna get us killed." With that, she lets the air escape between her lips and lays off until they hit a relative crawl at 75 mph.

Speed is objective and subjective at the same time. We all agree that the speed of light is fast, but 120 mph in a car may, or may not, be fast. One person's thrill ride is another person's beer run. Speed has everything to do with the magnification factor between you and the earth, you and the machine, and the machine and the earth. Jumbo jets, flying six miles in the sky at 550 mph don't feel or look fast, but 100 mph in an open A-V8 roadster

four inches off the pavement sure does. Proximity effect, wind, noise, curves, and sightlines all play a role in the sensation of speed ... a sensation of euphoria and fear at the same time. Adrenaline keeps us coming back for higher highs and faster speeds while technology enables the addiction.

Consider people born in 1880. For the first thirty years of their life they traveled on, or behind, a horse. If they took a train they might have hit 60 or 70 mph. By 1920, at the age of forty, they might own a car capable of 70 mph.

By the mid 1920s airplanes were over a hundred miles per hour and were flying across the Atlantic. By the late 1930s air and land speed records were over 300 mph. By the time these persons reach their mid-seventies, in the 1950s, they will have gone from the horse-and-buggy to witnessing aircraft faster than the speed of sound, and mass-produced automobiles capable of over 100 mph. If they made it to ninety they would see 200 mph stock cars and men on the moon. The technology feeds our desire and our desire pushes the technology.

We keep building these machines because speed will always keep us humans enthralled. Hot rods, dragsters, motorcycles, muscle cars, and carnival rides are all machines built to flow adrenaline. And in some cases to satisfy other desires: creative, sexual, or competitive. The common denominator is this question: "how fast is that thing?"

From the moment man realized that oil was more than just lamp fuel, and could be used to power a motor, he's been racing. It's the natural, competitive thing to do. In California, there was a natural phenomenon called dry lakes that offered early racers a large empty, relatively safe expanse on which to test their mettle and, their metal.

Even big Hollywood stars like Robert Stack raced at the dry lakes in the 1930's. In 1933, Zeppo Marx, driving a stripped-down supercharged Mercedes-Benz, raced Clark Gable's agent Phil Berg (in a stripped Duesenberg) for $10,000—a lot of money today let alone in Depression-era 1933. The onlookers included Carole Lombard, Al Jolson, Mae West and Clark Gable. Eddie Miller Jr., driving Berg's Mercedes, won the race and Berg collected big time.

Another guy there at the dry lakes was a young Wally Parks who, a few years later, in 1937, would be instrumental in the formation of the Southern California Timing Association (SCTA). Today, the SCTA still sanctions racing at El Mirage dry lake and, with its sister group Bonneville Nationals Inc. (racing on the Bonneville salt flats), the very roots of hot rodding were born. Men and women regularly go 200, 300 and sometimes 400 mph in wheel-driven vehicles of infinite shape and style. Wally, of course, went on to found the National Hot Rod Association (NHRA) in 1951 which is the world's largest motor sports sanctioning body. The NHRA continues to organize American drag racing at hundreds of tracks across the U.S.

After the founding of the NHRA, hot rodding exploded in hundreds of directions to include everything from the early hot rods and lakes racers to show cars, customs, modified pickups, rat rods and a gazillion other permutations—all of them acceptable as expressions of ingenuity and individualism. It's the freedom we continue to fight for, the freedom to seek speed.

Tony Thacker is executive director of the Wally Parks NHRA Motorsports Museum

RUN WHAT
YA BRUNG

On weekday nights dragstrips across the world host what is called a bracket race. In the parlance of the drag racing initiate it is also known as "run what ya brung". This is the time and place where an average person can bring any car to the strip and put the pedal to the metal with no fear of flashing lights in the rearview mirror.

This form of racing is called "bracket racing" because the cars are separated into brackets of those that run a certain time. For instance, all cars 14 seconds or slower generally would run alongside each other. At the end of the night it is not uncommon to see a 16-second grocery-getter racing against a full on 11-second race car. The 16-second car would get a head start and the first across the finish line wins. Unless the first car over the line does it too fast.

Every car must have a time written on the windshield that they hope to cover the quarter in. Let's take that 16-second car versus the 11-second car. Both cars feel like their times will be exactly 16 or exactly 11 seconds respectively. If the grocery-getter goes over the line first but does it in 15.99 seconds the car has "broken out" and is therefore disqualified and loses the race. The same goes for every car, if you run faster than your dial-in you are a loser. It is not as glamorous as true heads-up racing but it is fun all the same and about as close as any of us can get to the real deal.

Waiting to race is all part of the drag racing game.

Ice cream is also a part of a day's meal at the track.

BARRACUDA '66

This 1966 Barracuda is the famous Pandemonium match racer of the 1960s. Power is supplied by a nitro burning supercharged 392 Hemi. This car ran the quarter in the 9-second range at 177 mph.

Part of the color at any dragstrip is the announcer who keeps the audience up to date on the winners and losers. A good announcer will have a distinctive style and the ability to tell a good story about any of the racers on the track. Here is "Dragster Jeff" Jeff Crider on the mike at Famoso.

A 1970 'CUDA heats 'em up. Doing a burnout heats the rubber on the racing slicks for maximum traction at the start.

Left: Empty bleachers at Famoso. **Right:** The Knudson family with their 'Cuda at the Bakersfield Test and Tune.

Left: It takes two chutes to slow this DODGE CHALLENGER funny car. **Right:** "Code Red" CHALLENGER funny car melting some rubber. **Overleaf: (L)** This gasser failed to light and is being pushed back to the starting line.

Fans at the big end of the track get a view of the cars at top speed.

Above: Elapsed times and speeds are posted on these signs at the end of the quarter-mile. **Overleaf: (128/129)** A 1964 427-c.i. FORD THUNDERBOLT leaving the line hard and wheels up. **(130/131)** This gasser '37 CHEVROLET master deluxe coupe leaves the line at Bakersfield.

FUN FACTS ABOUT
TOP FUEL

1 - Blown nitromethane top fuel funny cars and dragsters make nearly 7000 horsepower.

2 - Top fuel dragsters run in the low 4-second range with top speeds of over 300 mph. A single cylinder in a blown nitro motor generates as much horsepower as an entire NASCAR engine does.

3 - A top fuel dragster accelerates from 0 to 100 mph in less time than it takes you to read this sentence.

4 - Top fuel drivers feel the same amount of gravitational force leaving the starting line as the astronauts do leaving the launchpad.

5 - When the chute is pulled at the end of a top fuel run, the force is equal to seven times the force of gravity.

6 - It takes nearly five gallons of fuel to travel a quarter mile in a top fueler. The entire run including burnout and staging requires 12 gallons of fuel at a cost of $16 per gallon.

7 - By the time a dragster travels 600 feet it has reached speeds in excess of 280 mph.

8 - The slicks on a top fueler are completely worn out in 4 to 6 runs.

9 - A top fuel dragster will outrun both a fighter jet and a formula 1 car for at least 4 seconds.

10 - If nothing blows up and the crew works for free, a top fuel run costs $1000 per second.

You can say the dry lakebeds of the Mojave Desert were where hotrodding all began and you'd not be far from the truth. At the same time, five hundred miles away on Utah's Bonneville salt flats a parallel development in top end desire was happening. On the lakes it was pure Southern California pre-war hotrodding, on the salt it was an international phenomenon.

Even though Utah's own son, Ab Jenkins, had set many records on the salt by the mid-thirties, the all-out record for speed was set in 1935 by a British man by the name of Sir Malcolm Campbell, at 301.12 mph. Back then no one gave serious thought to those crazies out in the California desert. Surely they couldn't hope to reach the incredible 300-plus mile per hour speeds of Campbell's "Blue Bird" in a fuel-injected jalopy? The ones who did believe were the lakes racers themselves and it was not lost on them that Bonneville would be where they could prove it. After much convincing the Southern California Timing Association (SCTA) got permission to use the salt flats from the Federal and the Utah state governments, along with certification for times achieved from the AAA. In 1949 the first Speed Week was held and a new era of American and International landspeed racing began.

On the salt, the racers finally had the room that the lakes could not afford to give, and the speeds quickly went up. Even though the price of speed also went up, the frequency of records held by largely self-financed operations went up too. It no longer took an entire country's treasury to go fast. As a result the level of ingenuity went up too.

By 1939 Englishman John Cobb had bested Campbell's 1935 record and fellow Brit John Eyston's 1937 record of 357.50 mph. After the war Cobb set the piston-engined, wheel-driven record at 394.19 mph. This record would stand for many years despite the best efforts of homegrown American hotrodders like Mickey Thompson, who in 1960 ran 406 mph in "Challenger I" but could not make a return run fast enough to catch the record, due to a broken driveshaft. It was not until the Summers Brothers ran their naturally aspirated, fuel-injected, quad 426 Hemi streamliner up to a two-way average of 409.344 in 1965 that the Americans could claim the honor of having the world's fastest vehicle.

The mid- to late-1960s saw an explosion in speed out on the salt as well as the lakes. Now roadsters were capable of 200 mph speeds and the lakesters were blazing over the 300 mark. Then along came the jet cars and the whole thing took a new twist as speeds went up over 500 mph. Art Afrons

and Craig Breedlove began to reach ever higher speeds in their jet cars and people began to wonder if a land-based vehicle could possibly break the sound barrier. Another question was whether or not these vehicles could really be considered cars and thus "fastest" became differentiated into jet-propelled, wheel-driven, and piston-engined categories. These categories are now further broken down by vehicle type and displacement of the engine as well as fuel type and body modifications. Jet cars no longer run at Speed Week but nearly every other sort of propulsion from electricity to turbines and diesels do run for records in their separate categories.

To cover all the achievements of the salt flat racers in this space would be impossible but a few notables bear inclusion: longtime competitor Al Teague who finally broke the Summers Brothers record in his "Spirit of '76" streamliner with a 409.986 mph two-way average. Nolan White who broke Teague's record at 413.156 mph and then died trying to break his own record in 2002. The Burkland family who broke Nolan's record with a two-way average of 417.020 mph. The late Don Vesco and his "Turbinator" turbine-powered streamliner which captured the wheel-driven landspeed record with a two-way average of 458.440 mph in 2001. Joe Amo who regularly runs over 240 mph on an un-streamlined motorcycle. The "Buckeye Bullet" electric streamliner from Ohio State University which ran 314.958 mph in 2004. While none of these vehicles has broken the sound barrier like the Thrust SSC jet car (763 mph), it is important to remember that all the above records are for wheel-driven vehicles.

2008 marks the 60th anniversary of Speed Week. The past few years indicate that interest in the event is growing. As we head further into this new millennium we will begin to see more and more vehicles with exotic fuels and power plants. Diesel technology will prove as fast as the fastest gasoline engines and hydrogen and electricity will become as common as the flathead was in the early '50s. Bonneville is the place where innovation and experimentation are rewarded and honored. Here on the salt, cars and bikes built and driven by competitors from all over the world will determine the vehicular future of speed and everyday transportation.

Left: The Burklands' "411" streamliner after a run at Bonneville. Both parachutes are visible as well as the hydraulically operated rear panels that swing out to produce additional drag. The fabrication skills of the Burkland family are plainly evident on this beautiful car. This streamliner is the fastest piston-driven car in the world, according to SCTA / BNI, at a two-way average of 417.020 mph. The car has gone as fast as 450 mph.
Right: Tom Burkland with his mother Betty and his father Gene.

"One Sixpack To Go" is a 1942 Chevrolet "aero" sedan running an old 302-c.i. "Jimmy Six" up to speeds of 155 mph.

Above: John Iannucci waits at the starting line in his GMC six-cylinder-powered 1950 sprint car. With the aid of fuel injection this car runs over 150 mph.
Overleaf: (L) Russ and Mark are crew members on the George Poteet and Ron Main "Eco Fire" streamliner. **(R)** Ty Baxter's handsome 1964 MERCURY COMET with 370-c.i. small block Ford power.

Above & Left: This '61 Ford Starliner is powered by a 359-c.i. Ford small block prepped by Roush Racing and is capable of 200 mph despite its lack of aerodynamic design. Driver Danny Burrow and the rest of the Camel Toe Racing crew are obviously blown away by the 199 mph performance of their 1961 Ford Starliner.
Overleaf: This long black line laid in the salt is what the drivers follow to keep them on course at Bonneville. In the distance is "Floating Island".

A chopped 1932 FORD coupe kicks up the dust on the dry lakebed of El Mirage in the Mojave Desert.

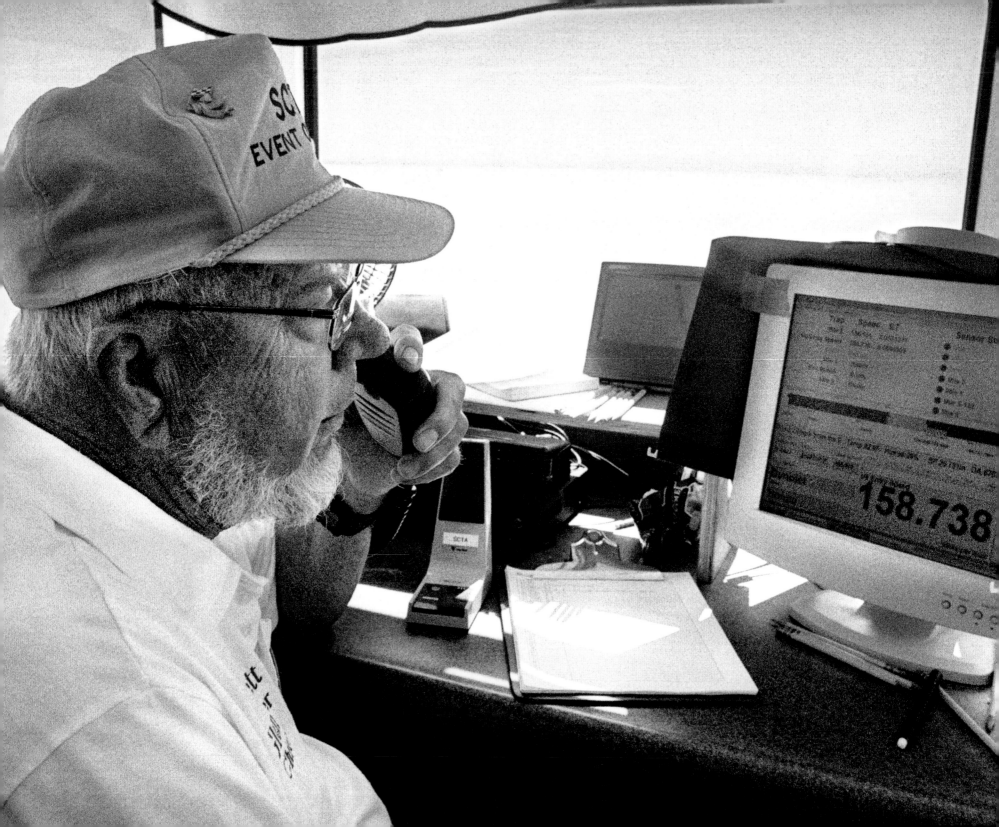

Crew members Nova and Randy Dugan give driver/nebulous theorist Jack Costella a helping hand as he replicates H. P. Mueller's victory handstand. In the background is the "Nebulous Theorem IV" streamliner with an 80 cc Honda engine. Jack just captured a record in the 'liner at 105 mph at El Mirage, in 2005 when this photo was taken. To date Costella and crew hold over 50 records.

250 mph

The blown lakester "Away Racing" with paraplegic driver Johnny Lee at the hand controls is churning the lakebed to dust at 250.043 mph. John is a member of the Muroc 200 MPH Club, as well as the Dirty Two Club at El Mirage and the Bonneville 200 MPH Club.

Left: Driver Inez Carlson on the El Mirage lakebed. **Right:** The Carlson family 1927 Ford roadster with a 1995, 180-c.i. Nissan V-6 engine.

Left: "Fast Freddy" Dannenfelzer's #44 blown fuel lakester is a regular at the lakes and at Bonneville. Fred runs various displacements of Hemis and in the "A" (440 to 500 cubic inches) category has a record with a two-way average of 355.109 mph. **Right:** Fred Dannenfelzer out at El Mirage.

The Wooden & Vaughn "AA" gas streamliner at El Mirage. This car currently holds the record for its class with a two-way average of 364.761 mph set in Bonneville 2004.

Here is the world's fastest four-cylinder-powered vehicle, the Costella/Yacoucci "Nebulous Theorem II". In 2006 Rick Yacoucci ran a blown 1520 cc engine on gasoline up to 360 mph with a two-way average of 352.525. Nothin' nebulous about that.

Rick Yacoucci.

Left: The "Sundowner" is a longtime veteran at the flats and regularly runs over 200 mph. In 1981 it was the world's fastest passenger car with a two-way average of 238.090 mph. This beautiful 1968 'VETTE is owned by David McKinney. **Right:** The cramped cockpit of the "Sundowner". The Large Aluminum tank holds extra water to cool the engine.

Left & Above: Crew chief Harry Garcia working on the Bakersfield Boys 1934 FORD, blown gas altered coupe. The iron 506 cubic inch Chevy took the coupe up to a 192 mph record when it was injected at Bonneville in 2006. The crew has spent seven years building up the car from swap meet and ebay scrounging. The guys like to call themselves the "one hit wonder". **Overleaf: (L)** '67 KARMANN GHIA driven by Rick MacLean, B. Boelcke and R. Holdener to many class records. Top speed was 151.415 mph in 2001. **(R)** Mike Cook Jr.'s '29 FORD roadster. This record holder has gone 245 mph.

This is the "Pumpkin Seed" streamliner originally built by "father of the belly tank" Bill Burke. Burke sold the car to Mickey Thompson and the car is now owned by Mickey's son Danny Thompson. Jim Travis restored the car and it now runs with an Ardun-headed flathead motor in the XXF streamliner class. With Danny Thompson at the wheel the 'liner holds a record set in 2004 with a two-way average of 253.503 on fuel.

Above: Jim Travis. **Overleaf:** Charles Reno waits at the starting line with his 800 horsepower 572-c.i. Rat motored roadster.

STYLE & SOUND

"Hot rod style" invokes speed, flash, and raw power. Under bright lights or into the negative space of a dark stretch of highway, the elements of the style are reflected in the functional beauty of a dry lakes racer or in the finessed sheet metal and deep hues of a meticulously crafted custom. And in between lie thousands of variations on the theme.

It begins with attitude. The true hot rod stance began with the need for speed on the dry lakes of Southern California. The lakes cars were generally open-wheeled roadsters that ran taller rear tires to permit higher top end speeds. The tall rear tires in conjunction with smaller front tires (and dropped front axles) lowered the nose. This forward "rake" defines hot rod. Complementing the "rake" would be a general lowering of the car, and if the car were a coupe,

its top would be chopped. Body panels were eliminated to save weight, in some cases leaving the engine wholly or partially exposed. These elements conspire to give a hot rod the feeling of motion at a standstill, and they serve the important function of making a hot rod faster under power.

To stress the feeling of motion you need some flash, like the paint schemes borrowed from the fighter planes of World War I and World War II that became part of the look. Flames raging from the nose and cowl give a literal interpretation of power and speed. Scallops, in contrast to body color, make a car appear to be exploding through color. In time, both accents became definitive style elements of hot rods as well as customs and street rods. Pin-striping the cars originated with the adornment of coaches, locomotives and fire equipment.

By the 1950s it blossomed into something more than the sign painter's hand-in-trade. With the talent and creativity of "Tommy the Greek" (Tommy Hrones), Ed Roth, and Von Dutch, striping became a free, though exacting, art form. Sometimes clean and understated, othertimes abstract or representational, the style the early stripers started is still practiced and expanded upon today … and not just on cars, but on everything from bowling pins to mass-produced tee shirts.

In the early days, the only things mass-produced about hotrodding were the cars the hotrodders used as raw material for their creations. Before mainstream acceptance, hotrodding was a definitive underground subculture. Now, hotrodding is a part of our culture that has spawned its own subcultures in art, music, and fashion. Most importantly, hotrodding has seen the development

Love & Hate

of a new subculture: one that builds modern interpretations based on the raw look of the earliest hot rods. Behind all of today's hype lies the truth that all this reworking of existing cars and engines, outright fabrication of body panels and parts, craft with paint and line, rebellion and genius make up "hot rod style". You know it when the engine fires, the tires bark and you feel the force of speed pressing you into the seat while the city becomes a blur.

That is when the mix explodes, and the sound races ahead of the flame, echoing off the crown to the roof of the chamber and back again. The exhaust valve opens and the sound escapes, pushing the air aside the way an enraged bull parts a crowd. At the end of the header its aggression is spent upon anything in its way. At full throttle the sound engulfs anything or anyone

within its grasp. It is time for sound, and long-term exposure can cause permanent damage. The addiction is manifested by the ringing in your ears in-between runs. Only the blissful decibels of uncorked exhaust can allay the maddening ring. The sound becomes a comfort. The way music can comfort a tormented soul.

Hot rods and music, or is it hot rods as music? Either way, rebel element meets rebel movement and forever they are joined at the hip. Dick Dale is wailin' out of a Woody. Wanda Jackson comes to life in the warm glow of the tubes in the radio of a '59 El Camino. Black Sabbath looms inside a smoke-filled black '70 Chevelle in the high school parking lot. Curtis Mayfield is slipping out of a "442" cruising a darkened city street. Link Wray shreds another speaker in a primered Model A Ford. A '64 Dart is shaking to the strains

of the Minutemen while the Stooges explode in a carpetless '69 Charger. Howlin' Wolf and Willie Dixon are making the card board speaker shake like jelly in the dash of a '40 Ford coupe and there is a little Led Zep in every Camaro.

Style and sound, like a hot rod, is power. The notes that die in the air around your head are not soon forgotten. They coalesce into any number of visual, olfactory or tactile memories. Sometimes the sound of an engine is just the sweet and simple sound of a loved one returning home. Power.

FEATURING
LUCHA LOCAS
WRESTLING

★ ★ ★

ROD POWELL ★★★

Many stripers do just that, they stripe and they generally will stripe you if you give them the chance. Rod Powell certainly stripes and stripes well. Will he stripe you? He might be apt to flame or scallop you if he was of the mind to paint a human body. This is because Rod is one of the masters of scallops and flames as well as pin-striping. The extension of striping into flames and scallops is no light matter.

Rod hits the bulls-eye squarely because he started in this mad business at the age of 14 on his dad's car back in Salinas in 1954. His work made the cover of *Rod and Custom* in August of 1968 and he's been developing and refining his designs ever since. Rod took the art of flames a step further in 1989 with his bold yellow flames on Tom Prufer's "Chop Shop Coupe" '32 FORD. In 1997 he released *King of Flames*, the definitive book on flame technique published by Featherston Productions.

The art in a Rod Powell flame is in its flow and motion. The composition draws the eye along the stem of the flame and back to the root, never detracting from the flow of the car. Not even on a car as unlikely as the white abalone-flaked 1960 IMPALA that Gary Howard built. Rod's flames, low on the car and between the wheels work in lavender with subtle scallops and draw your eye to the best features of the cars' and Gary's design. Nowadays Rod is working out of his shop in his hometown of Salinas. His art and his willingness to share his technique have inspired many. Today there are many stripers and flamers plying the trade and by Rod's admission there are "too many to list" whose work he admires. Thanks in many ways to the "King of Flames" himself, Rod Powell.

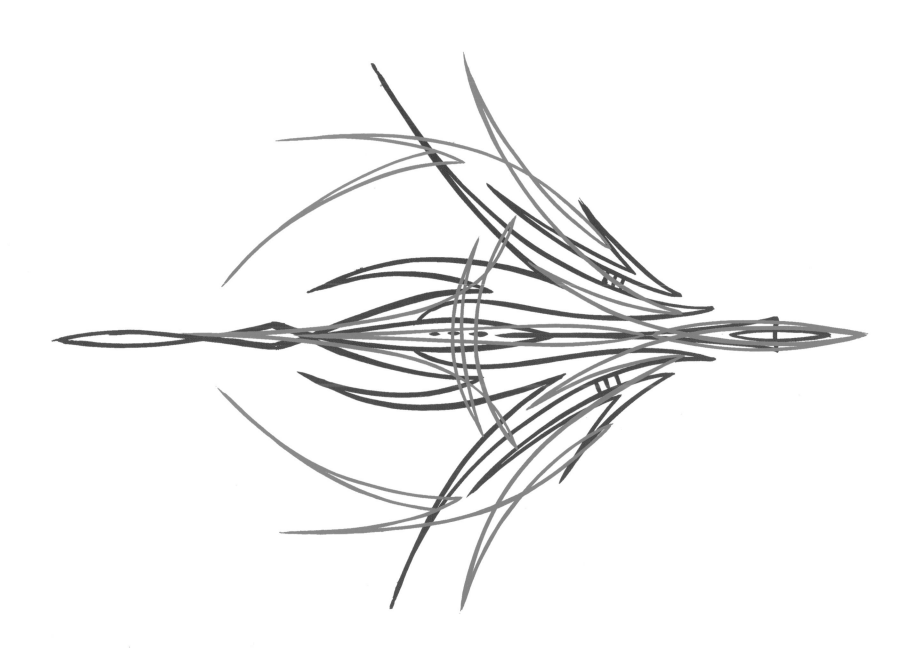

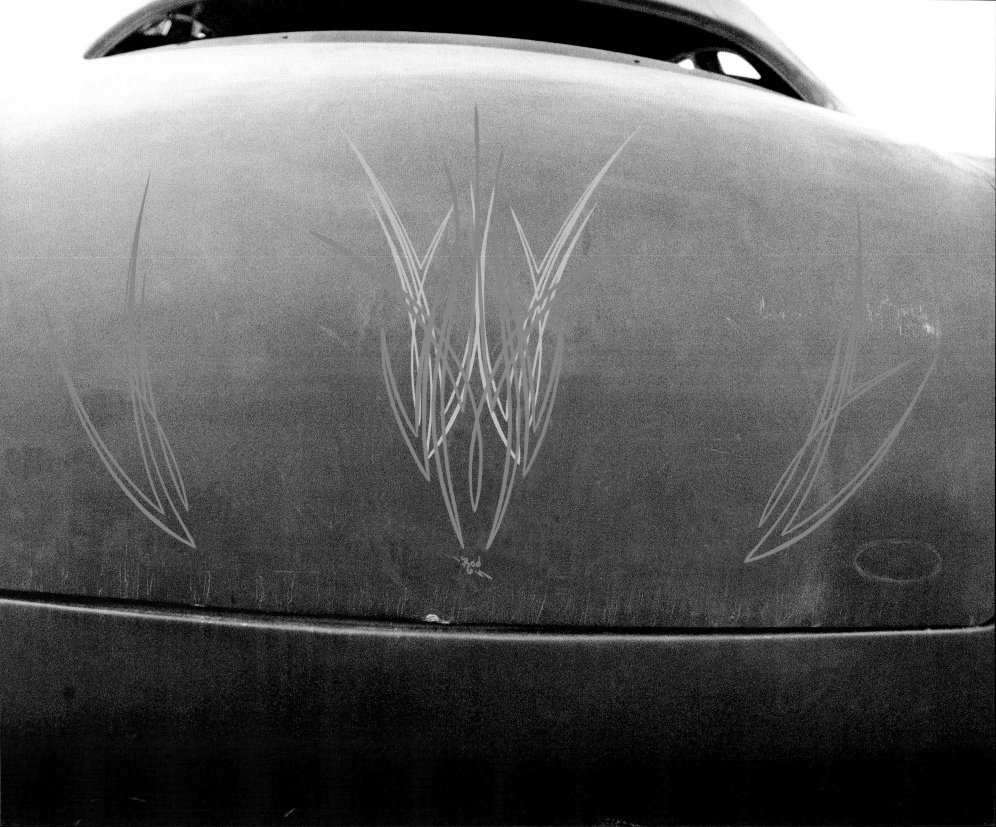

Tim at the Viva Las Vegas hot rod and custom culture get-together.

A flamed '55 Buick Century custom.

SS/AA 1968 BARRACUDA with a psychedelic fish scale paint job and gold leaf lettering.

Above: 1968 Ford Mustang GT 428 Cobra Jet. **Next 6 pages:** Examples of car lettering and flaming.

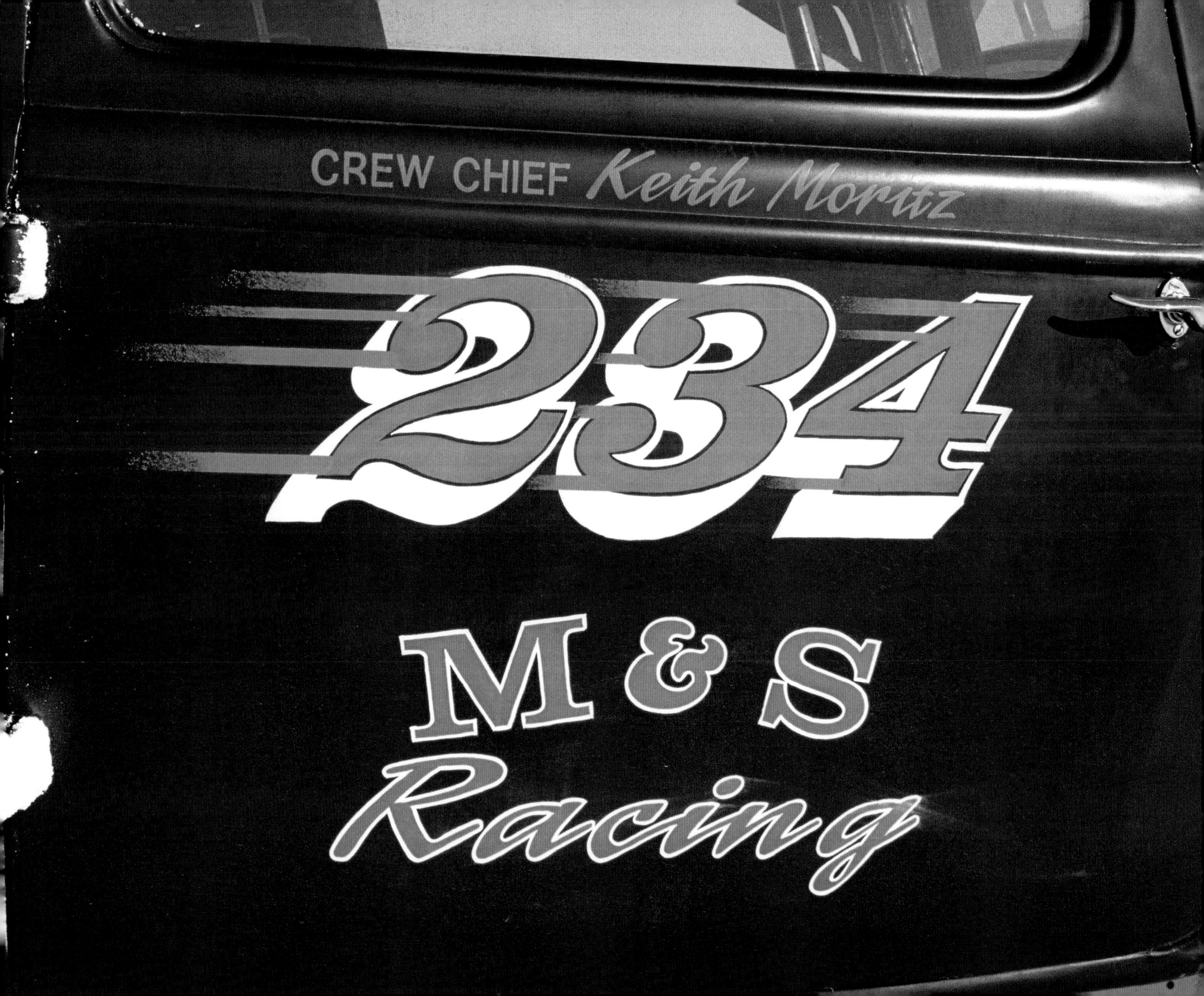
CREW CHIEF Keith Moritz
234
M & S
Racing

DIABLO ★★★

Pin-striping is an exacting and enduring form of hot rod and custom adornment. Ever since the infamous "Von Dutch" came on the scene and blew the lid off the moribund practice of simple adornment there have been hundreds of imitators. Most of these wannabees simply drop by the wayside or get blown into the weeds by others with more vigorous talent. "Diablo" Tom Herrera is one of the few who practice regularly at the top of the game.

Tom's style is of the bold line variety pioneered by "Von Dutch". Where Dutch's style could be playful or surrealist, Tom's is more on the ghoulish/satanic side of the coin. Horned and tailed bloody eyeballs, devils and outstretched batwings adorn any and all surfaces. Musical instruments are one of Tom's specialties and Anthony Vincent of The Rhythm Dragons is one of Tom's loyal customers. Tom's brushes hit the canvas too along with ink and pencil to create custom one-off pieces of art in the "lowbrow" vein. See, it's not only striping. Inspired by the friendship and support of Krazy Keith Adamo, Von Franco, and Rod Powell, Tom does logos, lettering and flames too.

Not content to just play with paint, Tom is a skilled fabricator with several builds under his belt and is head of the "Checs" car club in Bakersfield, California. When he's not scratching a Satanic itch he's dippin' into One Shot, cruisin' his '57 FORD wagon, or just plain hangin' with his wife Angie.

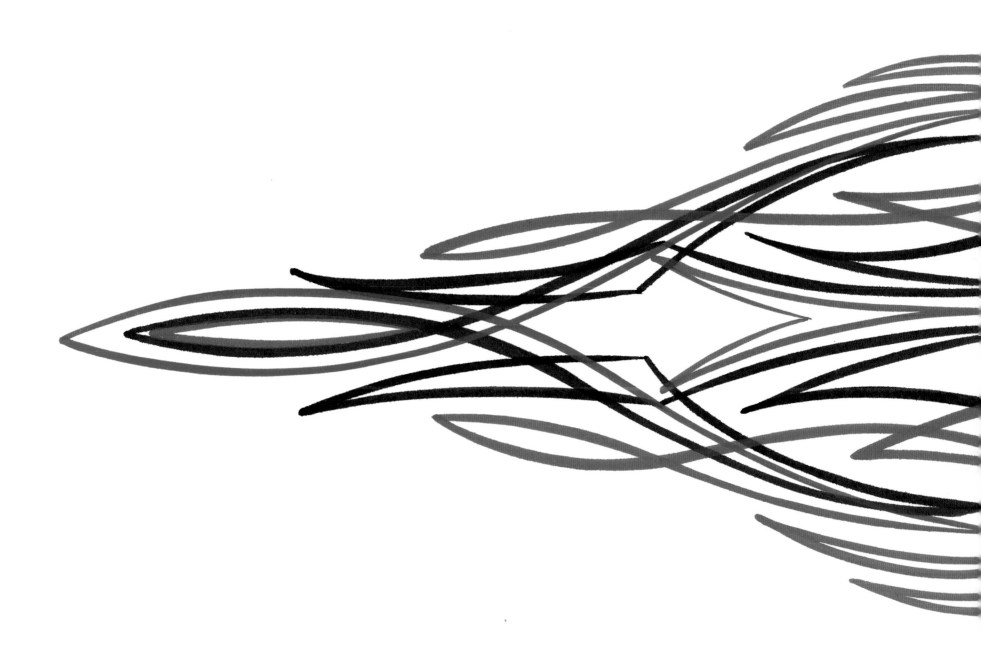

"DIABLO"

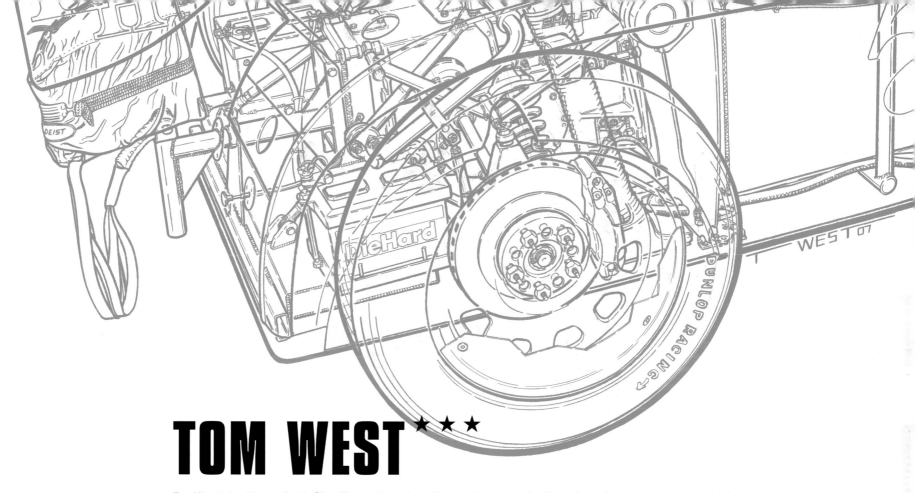

TOM WEST ★★★

Tom West is best known for his "See-Through" drawings. These intricately detailed X-ray views of racecars, hot rods, and daily drivers have earned Tom a place among the greats of the style such as William Moore and Steve Swaja. Tom's work has been published in *Popular Hot Rodding*, *Car Craft*, *Drag Racing USA*, Haynes repair manuals, and in Aurora, MPC and Revell model kits that he also had a hand in designing.

Cut-away drawing is an exacting combination of engineering, drafting and personal style. Since Tom was a 6-year-old boy in Quincy, Illinois he has always wanted to draw and design cars. In 1966, fresh out of high school, Tom began photographing at Irwindale (Orange County) and Lions dragstrips. His photo work got him involved with the hot rod and drag racing magazine trade and this soon led to drawing for the magazines. Inspired by drag racing, Steve Swaja, and William Moore, Tom's first published effort was a cut-away of the Herrera and Son's AA Gas AUSTIN race car that ran in the December 1968 issue of *Popular Hot Rodding*. He also landed the job held by Swaja and Moore doing the *Car Craft* "Cut-Away of the Month" series.

This began a period of Tom's life in which he attended engineering school in Michigan, held down a job at the GM plant, and photographed and drew cars. By the early seventies Tom moved to the East coast to take a job at Aurora model Kit Co., designing and acting as Research and Development manager. At Aurora Tom worked on designing the highly regarded 1/16 scale funny car kits known as the "Racing Scenes" series.

Between holding down jobs and relocating at the behest of model companies like MPC and Revell, Tom kept at the drawing whenever he could. One of his "greatest honors" is the cut-away he did for Don Garlits' "Swamp Rat XXX" Revell model kit that is on display at the Smithsonian along with the actual car. To date Tom has nearly 70 full-car "See-Through" drawings completed and is working on a history of hotrodding combining his own work with that of other illustrators. Tom has two grown children, Josh and Lauren, and lives in Southern California.

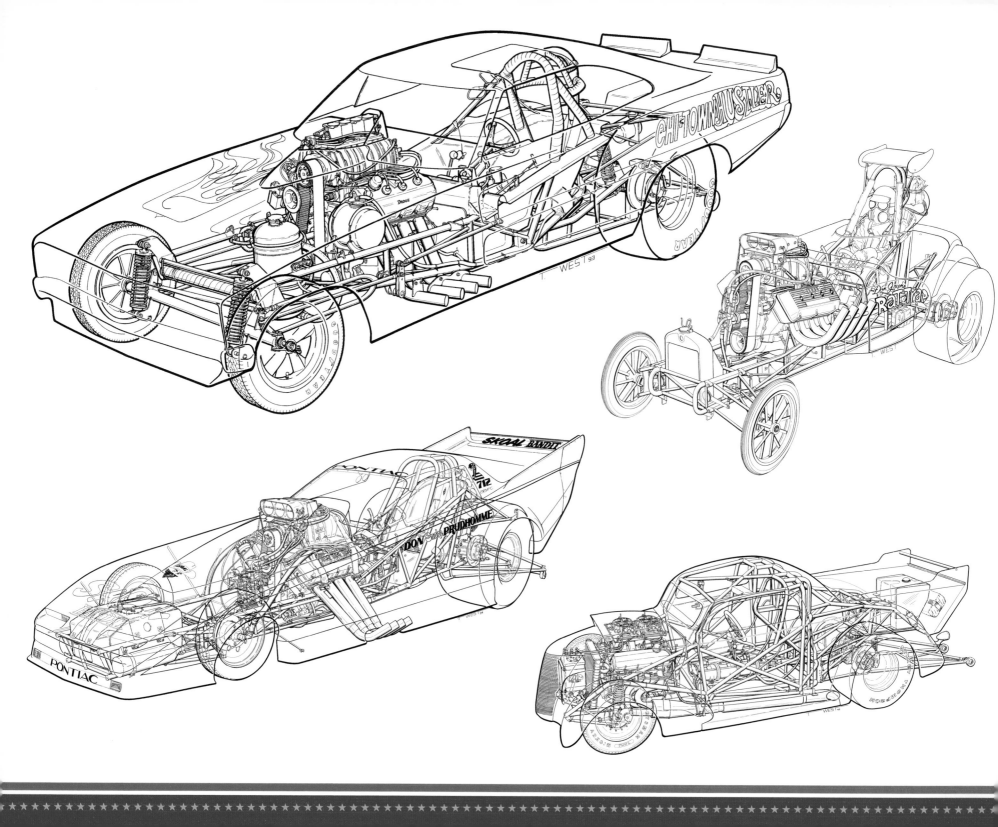

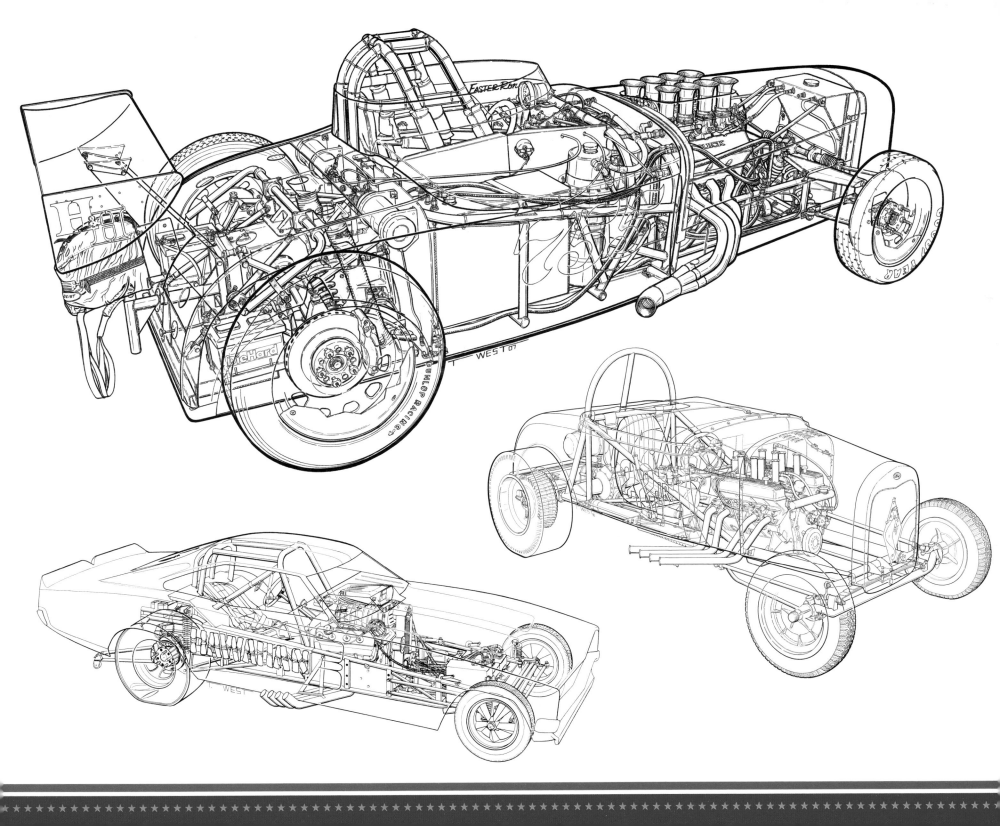

1966 Mustang Cobra Fastback

1970 Plymouth Barracuda

1964 Plymouth Sport Fury

1969 Plymouth Roadrunner

1967 Pontiac GTO

1971 Chevrolet Camaro

1967 Chevy Nova SS

1968 Dodge Charger

SID ★★★

Tattooing has been a part of the American subculture since the *Declaration of Independence* was signed. It is difficult to say exactly when tattooing became an integral part of hot rod culture. However, there is a parallel between the rise of a new counter-culture hitting the mainstream in the United States by the early 1990s and the rise of a new rockabilly-infused hot rod movement whose members are indeed heavily tattooed.

Since tattooing has gone fairly mainstream, the field has become a highly contested one and shops come and go. Sid's Tattoo Parlor, owned by Sid Stankovits, is the exception to the rule. Located in Santa Ana, California, Sid's has been around for 11 years. Quality tattoos with bold color and steady line work that sticks are the hallmark of Sid's artistry.

Sid was born in Anaheim, California in 1971 to a mother who is a painter and sculptor and a father perpetually into old cars and the music of the 1950s. Aside from tattooing, Sid is into painting and sculpting as well, and lists the 17th century painter Georges de La Tour as one of his influences right alongside the tattoo work of American master Sailor Jerry Collins. His daily drives are a '36 PLYMOUTH and a '28 FORD roadster. When he's not pushing ink into skin he's slapping an upright bass, or raising his children, Jonny, Aveline and June with his wife Jennifer.

KEY
TO MY
HEART

SAILOR'S ANGEL

RIP NAME

GAMBLING WITH THE LAW!

Sid's 5-window business coupe. 1936 Plymouth custom 3-window, chopped, '40 Chevy headlights, LaSalle grill, Ford taillights, 302 motor, air bags.

Anthony Castaneda of the Shifters Car Club with his Rothesque bubble-topped Model A called the "Brown Neck Bandit".

Left & Right: Jess in her garage with her Triumph motorcycle. Jess' house and garage are like a museum of vintage and custom culture artifacts.

Left & Right: Gearhead and musician Jake and his bedroom - living room - garage - studio with all the necessary ingredients to keep the inspiration flowing whenever the need arises.

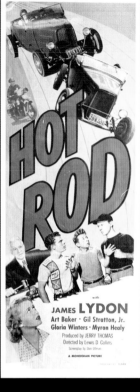

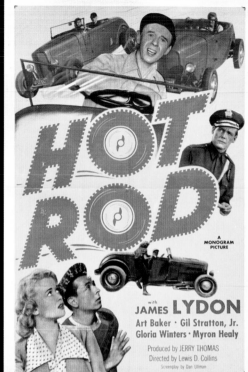

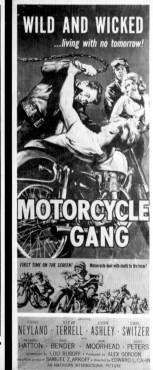

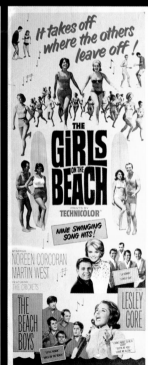

DAVID PERRY ★★★

David Perry began photographing as a youngster in Southern California. He never dropped the photographic thread even through his pomaded years as a musician in Pasadena. He began shooting the American underground hot rod scene in 1991. Perry's photographic vision first came to fame in the hot rod world with his book *Hot Rod*.

Hot Rod revealed a close look at the world of American underground hotrodding and lakes racing. What comes across is a dirty look that pays as much attention to the participants and their surroundings as it does to the cars themselves. High contrast and often times stark black-and-white imagery revealed David's skill as a printer as well as lensman. These images remain fresh and influential because they brought the viewer directly into the world contained within each frame.

Since *Hot Rod* David has been training his lens on two of his favorite subjects: beautiful women and automobiles. The first result was *Hot Rod Pin Ups*, a cocktail for the eyes, a mix of molls posed with iron that gets the job of "gow" done. A cleaner, more detail-oriented photographic look combines with David's eye for style and lighting in the pin ups series. 2008 finds David looking for as much trouble as he can find. A 1960 CHEVY BROOKWOOD wagon is tugging at him on one side of his coat and his son August on the other. Both projects are coming along nicely but August is the real gem and seems to be coming along a lot more quickly than the wagon. When he's not releasing a shutter, digging up work, or hanging out on a dry lakebed, he's at home in Vallejo, California taking care of business and August. We can all thank David's Uncle "Lucky" for handing David an 8mm Brownie movie camera back in 1969.

Amanda with a FORD MODEL A coupe.

Heidi with a 1925 CHRYSLER Model B70.

Jody at Salinas Boys Customs.

Sheri with a 1932 FORD roadster.

Gina with a 1928 FORD roadster.

Sabina standing in front of Lance Soliday's 1930 Model A with a '53 DeSoto Firedome Hemi under the hood. At Gold Coast Hotel, Viva Las Vegas.

Left: Sarah Louise with the Famoso Speedshop gasser. Right: Flaming tailpipes at the Viva Las Vegas show.

THE GOZZ ★★★

If the world gets any crazier there will be Bruce Gossett to turn to. Sure, his art is on the looney side and it's a better, not crazier world for that. While "spreading the madness" non-stop Bruce keeps his bullshit detector on high. This is the key to getting to know Bruce and his work. Born in St. Louis, Missouri, Bruce's stepfather was an automobile dealer. Throughout his years as a youth there was always "a killer ride in the garage". The young "Gozz" initially took up drawing and painting to get away from the car world and ironically wound up drawing and painting cars in Sacramento, California.

Mexican folk art, fire work packaging, comic art, automobilia, Americana, pulp themes and sex all figure into the Gossett frame. Arising from the wreckage of modern day "lowbrow", Bruce employs a rougher-hewn style and earthier palette than many of his contemporaries. The cleanest line is not always the fastest and Bruce knows when to put into the dirt. The ink and the dirt have been flying since 1999 when Bruce opened "Black Cat Press" with Ira Cowart. Silk-screening is one part of the trip, painting, drawing, striping and lettering is where "The Gozz" hits the gas and countersteers hard. All manner of media and surface are employed and even the demon airbrush can be found cradled in his fingers. Back to the bullshit detector. The detector pushes Bruce to create something original in a sea of sameness. The hand-drawn lettering, designs and imagery come straight out of his head and onto steel, paper and canvas. He is no stranger to the pain of the wrench either. A '54 Plymouth Savoy, '54 Plymouth wagon, '40 Chevy pickup, '37 Plymouth "Humpback" sedan, a '65 Fury, and his partner Yvette's '66 Pontiac Catalina and '65 'Cuda have all received bits of Bruce's flesh.

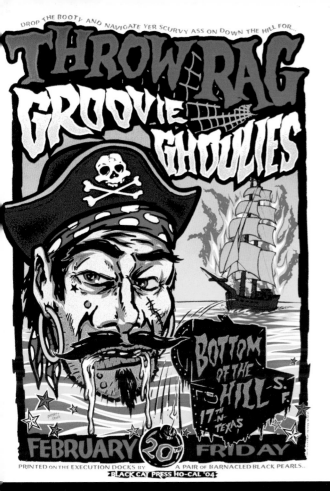

DROP THE BOOTY, AND NAVIGATE YER SCURVY ASS ON DOWN THE HILL FOR...

THROW RAG
GROOVIE GHOULIES

BOTTOM OF THE HILL S.F.
17TH 'N' TEXAS

FEBRUARY 20 FRIDAY

PRINTED ON THE EXECUTION DOCKS BY A PAIR OF BARNACLED BLACK PEARLS..
BLACK CAT PRESS NO-CAL '04

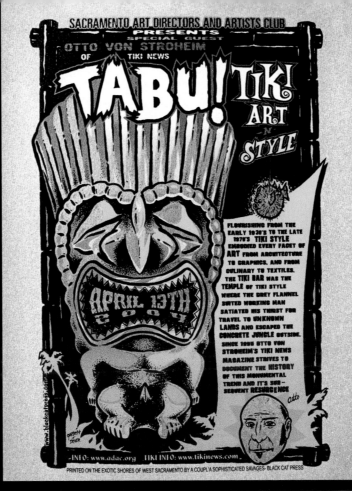

SACRAMENTO ART DIRECTORS AND ARTISTS CLUB
PRESENTS
SPECIAL GUEST
OTTO VON STROHEIM
OF TIKI NEWS

TABU!
TIKI ART 'N' STYLE

APRIL 13TH 2004

FLOURISHING FROM THE EARLY 1930'S TO THE LATE 1970'S TIKI STYLE EMBODIED EVERY FACET OF ART FROM ARCHITECTURE TO GRAPHICS, AND FROM CULINARY TO TEXTILES. THE TIKI BAR WAS THE TEMPLE OF TIKI STYLE WHERE THE GREY FLANNEL SUITED WORKING MAN SATIATED HIS THIRST FOR TRAVEL TO UNKNOWN LANDS AND ESCAPED THE CONCRETE JUNGLE OUTSIDE. SINCE 1995 OTTO VON STROHEIM'S TIKI NEWS MAGAZINE STRIVES TO DOCUMENT THE HISTORY OF THIS MONUMENTAL TREND AND IT'S SUBSEQUENT RESURGENCE

-INFO: www.adac.org   TIKI INFO: www.tikinews.com

PRINTED ON THE EXOTIC SHORES OF WEST SACRAMENTO BY A COUPL'A SOPHISTICATED SAVAGES- BLACK CAT PRESS

ZEKE

9 9 04

WITH
THE NITZ AND PSYCHOSOMATIC
10 PM
SACRAMENTO
21ST & L ST THE DISTILLERY CALIFORNIA DOWNTOWN

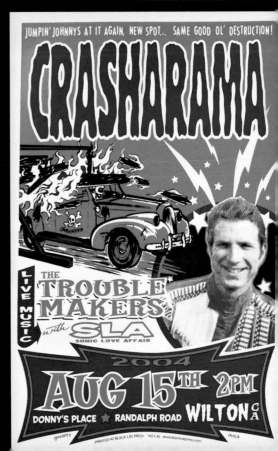

JUMPIN' JOHNNYS AT IT AGAIN, NEW SPOT... SAME GOOD OL' DESTRUCTION!

CRASHARAMA

LIVE MUSIC
THE TROUBLE MAKERS
with
SLA
SONIC LOVE AFFAIR

2004
AUG 15TH 2PM
WILTON CA
DONNY'S PLACE ★ RANDALPH ROAD WILTON CA

PRINTED AT BLACK CAT PRESS NO-CAL www.blackcatpress.com

NASHVILLE PUSSY
NOV 5TH
WITH BILLY GOATS GRUFF

POWERED BY PUSSY

8 PM
SACRAMENTO CALIF.
THE ROAD HOUSE

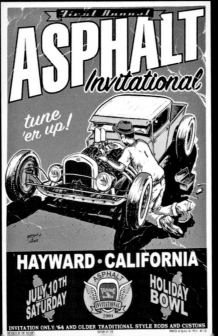

First Annual
ASPHALT
Invitational

tune 'er up!

HAYWARD · CALIFORNIA

JULY 10TH
SATURDAY

ASPHALT INVITATIONAL 2004

HOLIDAY BOWL

INVITATION ONLY! '64 AND OLDER TRADITIONAL STYLE RODS AND CUSTOMS

A NIGHT OF HYPNOTIC BAD ASS MISSISSIPPI BOOT STOMPIN' BOOGIE GROOVES

T-MODEL FORD

SPAM
KENNY BROWN

CEDRIC BURNSIDE
PAUL "WINE" JONES

26TH MAY 2004

AT POSSUM
THE JUKE JOINT CARAVAN TOUR

BLUE LAMP

DIRTY DONNY ★★★

Donny Gilles, alias "Dirty Donny" of Ottawa, Canada is a new psychedelic practitioner of the monster art style created by Ed Roth and Weirdo model box artist Bill Campbell. Donny's drawings and paintings create a playful world his monsters inhabit. Where others point a mean finger or go for the sheerly crass, Donny's monsters and miscreants seem to be having the kind of good time that you really want in on.

When "Dirty Donny" was a teenager he naturally gravitated towards the world of hot rods, muscle cars and old B-movie monster flicks. Donny also inhaled his share of glue while assembling Hawk, Weirdo, and Revell Ed "Big Daddy" Roth model kits. Time well spent in the underground rock and skateboard scene in Montreal led Donny to sign off of the installment plan and take the full plunge into his art.

Since moving to San Francisco he has sharpened his skills. His confident line work and attention to detail has allowed him to make a living doing what he loves most. Donny's goofy repertoire includes a design for Steve Caballero's new skateboard, Hellacopters and Demonics album cover art, custom pinball machines, and ceramic Tiki mugs. Donny is currently involved with a notorious mini-bike gang and is working toward putting his '69 SATELLITE into 440 monster wedge trim.

"DEMONS"

TWO-LANE TIKI'S

HRC

MAUI, HAWAII

POSTER POP

DIRTY DONNY

LUSURFERS

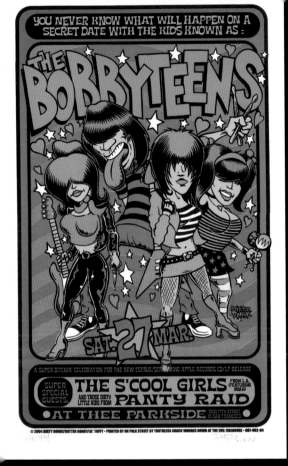

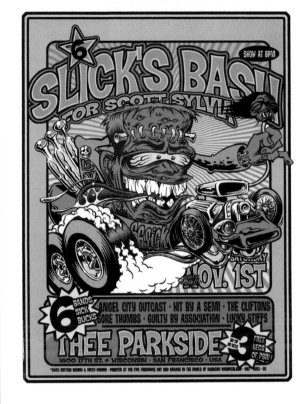

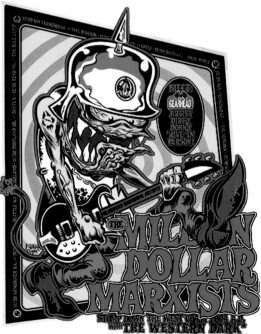

DICK DALE

For the hardcore surf aficionado there is nothing quite like a trip to the beach with "Misirlou" blasting out of the speakers and a perfect swell coming in. It's all the better if you happen to be driving a vintage station wagon with your long board hanging out the back window. Dick's music captures the essence of the experience because he knows firsthand what it is like to paddle out and catch a ride in the green room. Dick rode the waves in Southern California and played The Rendevous in Long Beach with other seminal surf bands like the Surfaris and Eddie & the Showmen. Dick and his Del-Tones released their first album *Surfers Choice* in 1962 and the die was cast.

The man is a legend and an inspiration to countless guitarists in search of that elusive muse called "tone". Any guitarist whose ever plugged into a Fender amp can thank Dick for his role in helping Leo Fender get that sound. Dick blew up nearly a hundred amps and countless speakers back in the day

and the feedback he gave to Leo Fender helped Leo refine the Fender sound. Together with the James B. Lansing speaker company they came up with a 100-watt guitar amplifier called the "Dual Showman" which pushed two specially-designed 15-inch speakers. Dick's ferocious playing and this amp brought about a whole new sonic era. The famous Fender reverb is also the result of a collaboration between Dick and Leo. Today Dick is still shredding the Stratocaster that Leo gave him and entertaining audiences worldwide with his inimitable surf rock sound.

TURBO A.C.'s

The Turbo A.C.'s came peeling out of the New York City rock n' roll rubble in 1995 and have kept the throttle mashed ever since. Using nothing but the best big block chords, valve bending tremolo and high RPM beats the A.C.'s have traveled the world and earned a devoted following of fans. Their endless touring would've flattened most mortal bands but not these NYC bruisers. After van rolls, spin-outs, squat-dwelling, and hardcore dues-paying, the boys are fit and ready to take on all comers with their intense, surf-inspired punk rock. Since 1996 they have released six LP's, issued numerous seven-inch singles and have been featured on countless compilations.

The live show is full of fun and fury and the Turbo A.C.'s deliver every time from parties to festivals. With over 10 years of experience the A.C.'s have found their songs being used in video games and on extreme sports television programming. Song lyrics frequently involve driving fast or singing the praises of high horsepower muscle cars. Sound collage fragments on the albums feature burning rubber, revving motors and dames in trouble. This love of cars and noir has endeared them to fans of the greaser punk movement and the A.C.'s are the perfect soundtrack for your TRANS AM at 100 mph. The band's name comes from the classic NYC gang film *The Warriors* and is a reference to a gang called "The Turnbull A.C.'s" that had a brief appearance in the film.

CHIP HANNA
& THE BERLIN THREE

When you're bouncing down the old dirt road in a hopped-up '36 Ford pickup on the way to the old swimming hole, Chip Hanna & the Berlin Three are the perfect soundtrack. Chip Hanna is a Louisiana boy living in the big city of Berlin making old time country sounds with a back-up band of Berliners who've done the requisite homework. Taking inspiration from country classicists like Merle Haggard and George Jones, Chip and the boys shake it up with a bit of Ramones and come out with a blackened slab of psycho-billy that'll get your boots working the floor in no time.

Chip played the drums in the hardcore punk band U.S. Bombs with legendary skater Duane Peters on vocals and has done time in One Man Army as well. Chip's punk (and the whole skateboarding ethos) experience serves him well on his country material where he assumes the role of frontman. His heartfelt delivery must be in his blood as his Mom sang country way back in the day in Pride, Louisiana. There is something about both genres, punk and country, that is unvarnished, immediate and true when done well and Chip gets it right every time. Chip Hanna & the Berlin Three have an LP called *Country Jamboree* out on "People Like You Records". It's a slab well deserving of a play on the old boombox when you're swinging out over the hole on the rope swing, tall boy in hand.

THE DEMONICS

The Demonics rip through the gears of surf-inspired punk rock like the ghost of Ronnie Sox charging for the finish line in a Hemi super stocker. Singer/songwriter Russ Wright formed the band in 1994 with Courtney Callahan on drums and Dez Mabunga on bass. Mid- and up-tempo songs focus on pop-culture, drag racing, girl chasing, surfing and skateboard mayhem. Without a single shred of pretension, but simply solid songwriting, Russ belts it out from his firsthand experience in the water, on the coping, under the hood and behind the wheel of his 1969 SUPER BEE.

That SUPER BEE has been the inspiration for many Demonics songs and in particular "Jesus Chrysler Super Stock" which tells the story of a pot smoking, drag racing savior. Russ has nearly completed the epic restoration of the BEE with an era-correct street racer hop-up that should put the streetable BEE into the 10-second range. The whole thing is beyond

obsession and Russ describes the car as his "religion". It's all about DIY, and the BEE and The Demonics are inextricably linked. With the help of friends the BEE has taken shape in Russ' garage at home just like all the homemade Demonics recordings have. Despite no new recorded output since 2002's *Ritual On The Beach*, The Demonics have reformed with Amy Cesari on drums and Joe Miller on bass. They have just released a "best of" 21-track compilation entitled *Hot Rod Pussy* and plan on recording new material just as soon as the new home studio is built.

THIS IS THE RACE THAT NEVER ENDS

The first pair of staging yellows are lit, and the car lurches forward to the start position. The next two lights come up, the revs screaming now. On the third yellow, just before green, the brake is released and the right foot stomps down furiously.

In the next lane the same thing is happening.

The left fender rises and the car lifts on its haunches. Like a bolting cheetah. The slicks grab hold after a brief smoke-inducing spin, and the race is on. Two seconds later, the left foot smacks the clutch and the shifter is thrown violently into second. The right foot pins the pedal to the floor. The car bucks, grabs the track and moves out.

In the next lane, a fender looms in the periphery.

Both engines scream in the 8000 rpm range. The sound is deafening inside the helmet. Barely 6 seconds go by and the car is hot, sweat fills and burns the eyes, blurring the driver's vision.

On the right, the fender is still threatening, barely edging ahead.

The shifter is thrown again and the fender falls away, almost to the passenger door now. The possibility of a win brings an extra shot of adrenaline. The tach flashes over 8 grand, and with a final shift we are in fourth gear. Everything is burning hot metal, headers are glowing. The car is shaking like a lover on the verge.

On the right, the fender lurks again, in slow motion. At over a 120 mph it is gaining steadily.

He silently coaxes the car like a jockey might speak to his horse. Nothing matters now, but passing the line first. The right foot lifts and a relative quiet overcomes the car and driver. The boom of the chute is left behind and the car slows.

To the outsider, the affair borders on ludicrous, a state of arrested development. But you know better. There is so much more to it. Knowledge and experience gained, skills and friends acquired, memories and the chemistry of the brain delivering the goods when the engine screams.

This is a race that never ends. It might look and sound different tomorrow but as long as there are vehicles to drive and human beings to race them there will always be a contest somewhere on this Earth.

THE SUPPORT OF THESE PEOPLE HELPED BRING THIS BOOK TO LIFE:

KEVIN THOMSON
TOM WEST
MICHAEL WITTLING
TONY THACKER

AN INCOMPLETE LIST OF THOSE WHO HAVE SUPPORTED AND INSPIRED ME OVER THE YEARS

My Parents who made this happen • Jens Peter Mollenhauer • Kevin Thomson & Pat • Steve and Bethany Reyes • JoAnn and Gregg Carson and the SCTA
Tony Thacker & Greg Sharp NHRA Museum • Andreas Siebert • Jan Clasen • Henry Astor • Tom & Angi Herrera • Anthony and the Shifters • Isaac • Vanessa
Rod Powell • Heiko Henschel • Klaus Merz • Fred Dannfelder • Jack Costella • Bruce Gossett • Ira & Ivet • Simone Schillo • Malte & Sheba • Jen-Lee
Jason Hamilton • Johnny • Markus Hübner • Johnny Crasharama • Steffi Thon • Dirty Donny • Gero • Drew Wiederman • Kennedy Brothers • Mary Perry
David Perry • Rod Welch • Cole Foster & Susan • Ron Main • Scott Mugford • Marc • Kurt Stockman • Maureen Bach • Wayne • Michael Matzke • Jim Jensen
Craig Hoelzel • Kenny Loewen • Danny • Gulio • Rick Merc • Gearhead • Chris Piaggi • Nikki Martin • Castrol • Jack Williams • Matt Marshall • Tim
Chip Hanna • Turbo A.C.´s • The Demonics • Dick Dale • Earl Plahang • Hotwheels • Fred Dannenfelzer • Cisco • Brandon • Malte Rehde • Dan • Miki Bunch
Garry and Joann • Jessica Ward • Dave Parker • Mimi • Rick Yacoucci • Peter with the Bus and Inke • Gene Winfield • Tommy Ivo • Carnetto • Mike Lugo
Sabine Muschter • Marco Almera • Dirk von Manteuffel • Motoraver Magazine • Christian Böhner • Tanja Ferkau • Michael Hollander • Gussy • Don Massey
Sid & Jennifer Stankovits • Art Croft • Dickies • Mike and Rob Cambell • Ray Petersen • Jack Costella • Eleanor Garcia • Geoff and Sharan
Harry Brack • Gene Winfield • Jon Bastian • People like you • Bitzcore • Aliennatch • Dan Druff • Bill Groak • Eva Pech • Pork Pie • Chrisi Weird Word
Steve & Bethany Reyes • Otto Ryssman • Dee & Ray Brown • Rust Magazine • Goodguys • James Dean • Arne Weychardt • Philip Kurzenberger
Tim Lötzerich • Esther Durtschi • Michael Wittling / Gold GmbH • Anika Heusermann • David Lopes • Mo & Gingko Press

THANK YOU TO EVERYONE WHO STOOD UP FOR THIS IDEA WHICH TOOK ME 10 YEARS TO REALIZE.

001

002 / 003
Belly tank at Bonneville.

Speedseekers Logo
Photo & logo design by Alexandra Lier.

004 / 005
Contents.

006 / 007
Don Prudhomme and Tom McEwen face off in
the early 1970s.

"HOT WHEELS" and associated trademarks
and trade dress are owned by and used under
license from Mattel, Inc. ©2008 Mattel, Inc. All
Rights Reserved.

008 / 009
History

010 / 011
History foldout.

"HOT WHEELS" and associated trademarks
and trade dress are owned by and used under
license from Mattel, Inc. ©2008 Mattel, Inc. All
Rights Reserved.

012 / 013
History foldout.

014 / 015
Photos by Ray Brown.

016 / 017
Photo by Otto Ryssman.

Vintage magazines. Wally Parks NHRA
museum collection.

018 / 019
Photo Wally Parks NHRA museum collection,
Greg Sharp.

020 / 021
Photos by Tom West.

022 / 023
Photos by Steve Reyes.

Old drag racing magazines. NHRA museum
collection.

024 / 025
Photos by Tom West.

026 / 027
Photos by Tom West.

028 / 029
Photos by Tom West.

030 / 031
Photos by Tom West.

032 / 033
Photo by Tom West.

034 / 035
Shirley Muldowney vs. Terry Capps, Indy 1979.
Photo by Tom West.

"Big Daddy" Don Garlits' fire burnout, at IHRA
Winternationals, Lakeland 1972. Photo by Steve
Reyes.

036 / 037
Photo by Alexandra Lier.

Photo Tom West collection.

038 / 039
Photos by Steve Reyes.

Photos by Tom West.

040 / 041
Photos by Steve Reyes.

042 / 043
Photos by Tom West.

044 / 045
Photo Tommy Ivo collection.

Photo by Tom West.

046 / 047
Photos by Tom West.

048 / 049
Garage

050 / 051
Photo by Klaus Merz.

052 / 053
Photos by Alexandra Lier.

054 / 055
Kevin at Shifters Car Club.

Chopped and channelled '32 FORD Tudor at Harry's Garage (New Zealand). Photos by Alexandra Lier

056 / 057
Photos by Alexandra Lier.

058 / 059
Photos by Alexandra Lier.

060 / 061
Photo by Alexandra Lier.

062 / 063
Salinas Boys with their '36 FORD coupe.
Photo by Alexandra Lier.

064 / 065
David Haas' streamliner at SoCal Speedshop.
Photo by Alexandra Lier.

066 / 067
Photos by Alexandra Lier.

068 / 069
Photos by Alexandra Lier.

070 / 071
Photos by Alexandra Lier.

072 / 073
Photos by Alexandra Lier.

074 / 075
Pin up © by David Perry.
Photo by Alexandra Lier.

076 / 077
Photos by Alexandra Lier.

078 / 079
Photos by Alexandra Lier.

080 / 081
Photos by Alexandra Lier.

082 / 083
Photos by Alexandra Lier.

084 / 085
Photos by Alexandra Lier.

086 / 087
Photo by Alexandra Lier.

Illustration by Bruce Gossett.

088 / 089
Anthony working on a piece.

Anthony's garage.
Photos by Alexandra Lier.

090 / 091
Vintage magazine overview. NHRA museum collection / Hop Up magazine collection.

092 / 093
Before and after paint job of Don Prudhomme's famous 'CUDA funny car. Photos by Dave Parker.

094 / 095
Photos by Alexandra Lier.

096 / 097
Photos by Alexandra Lier.

098 / 099
Photos by Alexandra Lier.

100 / 101
Speed

102 / 103
Photo by David Perry.

104 / 105
Doorslammers, stock-bodied passenger cars, line up in the staging lanes to race the quarter-mile. Photo by Alexandra Lier.

106 / 107
CHEVY MONZA frying the baloney in preparation for a race. Photo by Klaus Merz.

Photo by Drew Wiedermann.

108 / 109
Photos by Klaus Merz.

110 / 111
1968 super stock Hemi 'CUDA at Thunder Valley raceway, Tennessee.

Photos by Alexandra Lier.

112 / 113
Photos by Alexandra Lier.

114 / 115
Photos by Alexandra Lier.

116 / 117
Nostalgia drag racers at the Marchmeet. Photos by Alexandra Lier.

118 / 119
Funny cars before the start. Photos by Alexandra Lier.

120 / 121
Colorful paint jobs and lettering.

Photos by Alexandra Lier.

122 / 123
Photos by Alexandra Lier.

124 / 125
Photos by Alexandra Lier.

126 / 127
Photos by Alexandra Lier.

128 / 129
Photo by Alexandra Lier.

130 / 131
Photo by Alexandra Lier.

132 / 133
Photo by Drew Wiederman.

134 / 135
Top fuel fun facts.

136 / 137
Modern fuel funny cars now run just under five seconds and over 300 mph.

Top fuel burnout. Photos by Alexandra Lier.

138 / 139
Jet engine cars put on fiery exhibition runs and are capable of 300 mph speeds. Photo by Klaus Merz.

140 / 141
Landspeed intro.
Photo by Alexandra Lier.

142 / 143
Photos by Alexandra Lier.

144 / 145
Photos by Alexandra Lier.

146 / 147
Photos by Alexandra Lier.

148 / 149
Chief Starter Jim Jensen at Speed Week.

The "Grim Reefer" is a 1941 NASH 600 coupe with a 1951 Ford flathead V-8 displacing 276-c.i. Photos by Alexandra Lier.

150 / 151
Photos by Alexandra Lier.

152 / 153
Photo by Alexandra Lier.

154 / 155
Crew members of the "Salty Dog" with driver/ owner John Drake.

The windscreen on the "Salty Dog" roadster displays specific and important instructions for the driver. Photos by Alexandra Lier.

156 / 157
Photos by Alexandra Lier.

158 / 159
Photos by Alexandra Lier.

160 / 161
Bonneville Chief Timer Glen Barrett. Photos by Alexandra Lier.

162 / 163
Photos by Alexandra Lier.

164 / 165
Photos by Alexandra Lier.

166 / 167
Photos by Alexandra Lier.

168 / 169
Photos by Alexandra Lier.

170 / 171
Photos by Alexandra Lier.

172 / 173
Photos by Alexandra Lier.

174 / 175
Photos by Alexandra Lier.

176 / 177
The first diesel to do over 300 mph. Roy Lewis' diesel streamliner. Photo by Alexandra Lier.

SCTA logo.

178 / 179
Robert at the salt flats, a hardcore fan.

"End of the Road Gang" campsite at Bonneville. Photos by Alexandra Lier.

180 / 181
Photos by Alexandra Lier.

182 / 183
Photo by Alexandra Lier.

184 / 185
Style & Sound

186 / 187
Vanessa wrestles for the Lucha Locas wrestling team, at car shows and nightclubs in California. Photo by Alexandra Lier.

188 / 189
Artist Rod Powell. Photo by Alexandra Lier.

190 / 191
Pin-striping by Rod Powell. Photo by Alexandra Lier.

192 / 193
Photos by Alexandra Lier.

194 / 195
A front-engine nostalgia dragster with a retro styled paint job.

CHEVROLET V8 – 396 turbo jet 385 hp. Photos by Alexandra Lier.

196 / 197
Photos by Alexandra Lier.

198 / 199
Lettering on Bonneville cars. Photos by Alexandra Lier.

200 / 201
Lettering on Bonneville cars. Photos by
Alexandra Lier.

202 / 203
Classic '60s style lettering and flaming fish
scales on a '68 Hemi 'Cuda. Photos by Klaus
Merz.

204 / 205
Artist Tom Diablo Herrera.
www.diabloartwerks.com

Photo by Alexandra Lier.

206 / 207
Diablo's pin-striping.

208 / 209
Tom Herrera's custom T-Bird with panel
painting and striping by Diablo himself.
Photo by Alexandra Lier.

210 / 211
Artist Tom West.
www.milestonedg.com

Photo by Alexandra Lier.

212 / 213
"See-Through" drawings by Tom West.

214 / 215
Photos by Alexandra Lier.

216 / 217
Artist Sid Stankovits.
www.sidstattooparlor.com

Photo by Alexandra Lier.

218 / 219
Tattoo "flash" by Sid.

220 / 221
Tattoo "flash" by Sid.

Photo by Alexandra Lier.

222 / 223
Jen Lee's tattoos.

Jen Lee in her garage in Long Beach,
California.
Photos by Alexandra Lier.

224 / 225
Photo by Alexandra Lier.

Illustration by Bruce Gossett.

226 / 227
Photos by Alexandra Lier.

228 / 229
Photos by Alexandra Lier.

230 / 231
Car Movie Posters. Ron Main collection.

Cisco Aguilar driving through San Diego.
Photo by Alexandra Lier.

232 / 233
Fuzzy Dice in a 1950 Ford shoebox with a
100 hp flathead under the hood.

Shrunken head in a 1960 F100.
Photos by Alexandra Lier.

234 / 235
Custom interior.

Custom interior with low-rider style chain
steering wheel. Photos by Alexandra Lier.

236 / 237
Scott Mugford's 1968 Plymouth Fury Station
wagon with Frankenstein head as hood
ornament.

Checs car club plaque on Tom's '59 Ford
Thunderbird. Photos by Alexandra Lier.

238 / 239
Artist David Perry.
www.davidperrystudios.com

Photo by Alexandra Lier.

240 / 241
Photos by David Perry.

242 / 243
Photos by Alexandra Lier.

244 / 245
Artist Bruce Gossett, "The Gozz".
www.blackcatpress.com

Photo by Alexandra Lier.

246 / 247
Bruce Gossett poster art.

248 / 249
Bruce Gossett poster art.

Gossett's '54 Plymouth Savoy.
Photo by Alexandra Lier.

250 / 251
Artist Dirty Donny.
www.dirty donny.com

Photo by Alexandra Lier.

252 / 253
Art by Dirty Donny.

254 / 255
Dirty Donny drawing. Photo Dirty Donny
collection.

Poster art by Dirty Donny.

256 / 257
Dick Dale.
www.dickdale.com

Photo by Alexandra Lier.

258 / 259
Turbo A.C.'s.
www.turboacs.com

Photo by Alexandra Lier.

260 / 261
Chip Hanna.
www.chiphanna.com

Photo by Alexandra Lier.

262 / 263
The Demonics.

Photo by Alexandra Lier.

Concept, Photography & Design: Alexandra Lier
Edited by Anika Heusermann

Illustrations:
Bruce Gossett - www.blackcatpress.com
Dirty Donny - www.dirtydonny.com
Sid Tattoo - www.sidstattooparlor.com
Tom West - www.milestonedg.com
Harry Brack - www.scare-skate.com

Additional photography:
David Perry • Klaus Merz • Drew Wiederman • Dave Parker

Historical Pictures by:
Tom West
Steve Reyes - www.reyesontour.com
NHRA Museum • Otto Ryssman • Ray Brown

First published in the United Kingdom in 2009 by
Thames & Hudson Ltd, 181A High Holborn,
London WC1V 7QX

www.thamesandhudson.com

© 2008 Alexandra Lier
www.speedseekers.de

Text © 2008 Kevin Thomson

Original edition © 2008 Gingko Press, Inc.
5768 Paradise Drive, Suite J
Corte Madera CA 94925
USA

British Library Cataloguing-in-Publication Data
A catalogue record for this book is available from the British Library

ISBN: 978-0-500-51465-8

Printed and bound in China

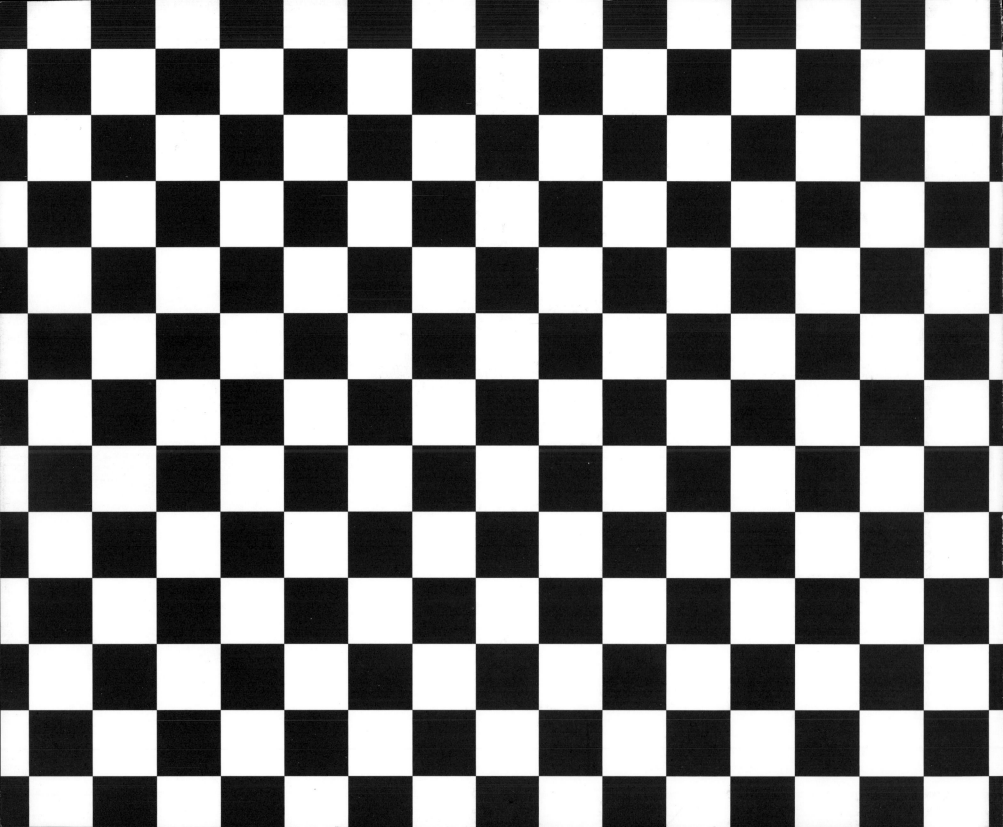